Answers to Your Real Estate Questions:

Smart and Profitable Real Estate Investing for Canadians

Answers to Your Real Estate Questions:

Smart and Profitable Real Estate Investing for Canadians

S. M. Herzog

iUniverse, Inc.
New York Lincoln Shanghai

Answers to Your Real Estate Questions:
Smart and Profitable Real Estate Investing for Canadians

Copyright © 2007 by S. M. Herzog

All rights reserved. No part of this book may be used or reproduced by any means, graphic, electronic, or mechanical, including photocopying, recording, taping or by any information storage retrieval system without the written permission of the publisher except in the case of brief quotations embodied in critical articles and reviews.

iUniverse books may be ordered through booksellers or by contacting:

iUniverse
2021 Pine Lake Road, Suite 100
Lincoln, NE 68512
www.iuniverse.com
1-800-Authors (1-800-288-4677)

Because of the dynamic nature of the Internet, any Web addresses or links contained in this book may have changed since publication and may no longer be valid.

The information, ideas, and suggestions in this book are not intended to render professional advice. Before following any suggestions contained in this book, you should consult your personal accountant or other financial advisor. Neither the author nor the publisher shall be liable or responsible for any loss or damage allegedly arising as a consequence of your use or application of any information or suggestions in this book.

ISBN: 978-0-595-44318-5 (pbk)
ISBN: 978-0-595-88648-7 (ebk)

Printed in the United States of America

CONTENTS

ACKNOWLEDGMENTS

I wish to express my appreciation and gratitude to my two editors David Bernardi and Jan Howarth. I am also very thankful to the many friends who supported me to finalize this book.

PREFACE

Why did I write this book? As I come from an immigrant family and have a multicultural education, a critical analysis of the Canadian system of how to invest in real estate came quite naturally. When I was only eleven, my family immersed me into the Canadian culture. Later, as a young adult, academic excellence in high school lead to McGill University in Montreal and from there to the ESADE Business School in Barcelona, Spain, and finally to the HEC Business School in Paris, France, for higher studies in business and management.

With this kind of international background, I found it a challenge to compete with my Canadian friends and peers when I returned from abroad to Canada. Now I had to anchor myself and put roots down somewhere in this fascinating, wonderful country. Having the freedom to choose where to go and the opportunity to establish solid fundamentals to pursue a happy life, I soon became aware of the fantastic opportunities in the real estate market. Careful with money and value oriented, I kept my eyes wide open. Before I arrived at conclusions and made decisions, I embarked on intensive studies of the Canadian real estate market, and plotted successful strategies. Learning from the experience of others, as well, proved to be a valuable tool.

I vigorously studied the subject for years and am happy and successful with my real estate investments. My intention is to pass on to you a great deal of the valuable information I have learned over the years. You can learn it in the very short time it takes to read this book!

INTRODUCTION

These days consumers are bombarded with a special type of real estate advertising: the chic, appealing, and provocative real estate ads that have become omnipresent. Have you ever wondered how easily your attention is caught by these shiny ads and glossy brochures? They follow us wherever advertising can reach us—they're even on the bus! They intrigue us with their bright colours, fantastic designs, and fabulous living promises. "Don't we all want to climb the ladder to success?" they ask. Of course we do!

The fantastic designs of the ads invite us to wander through tastefully tiled entrances in various colours of slate; to glimpse into designer kitchens, and taste the comfort of modern, all inclusive living spaces; to peek into even more luxurious marble bathrooms. Interior decorators have done a marvelous job by using professionally matched color schemes throughout and including extra-large stainless steel appliances, kitchen islands with granite countertops, and cozy electric fireplaces. Some of the new projects are landmarks built as urban renewal projects in choice locations with prestigious designs. Wouldn't you like to move into one of these lovely new places? Don't you wish you could call one of them your own?

All this is within reach, we are told: the better life and, with it, a demonstration of our success. Just go for it! With their suggestive and highly stylish advertising, developers promote the idea that, in our modern world, we again can live and work in city centers and be within reach of all the action, yet still be close to nature. Mountain views, lake views, and sea views are at the top of the list of what speaks to our senses, with artificial waterways and plazas with fountains coming next in the line of features that delight the eye of the prospective buyer. The splendid colours of the rising sun or a gorgeous sunset, viewed from your living room or your balcony, affect your mood and instill the desire to own such splendour. Or, maybe a view over autumn-coloured wooded parkland is the trigger point that will get you to buy. If the environment tops your list of values, then developments with eco-friendly values in a healthy and safe environment and consideration for "green" technology might be for you. And then there is the newly promoted idea of the European village, with all amenities such as restaurants, coffee bars, and a grocery store, as well as a pharmacy and perhaps a doctor's office all in the same complex or within walking distance—and near to public transit systems.

It is fun to look at all the new projects and get a feeling for what is out there. The information can be helpful as you make up your mind about what is right for you and before making an informed decision. It is wise to expose yourself to a variety of locations and styles so that you can make an educated decision about where and how stylishly you want to live, and how to balance these ideas within a sound financial framework. Knowing what you want and knowing what you can afford are major steps towards ownership of real estate.

Also, decide if you are keen on buying a project that is in one of the various phases of development. This often enables you to make some choice in the materials and colour schemes used in decorating. Or, you could prefer to buy only once the project is finished, when you can thoroughly inspect the site and be assured you won't have to bother with possible delays in completion time, or other possible setbacks or surprises.

A totally different matter to consider is your personal flexibility and your outlook on the future. Will you move in and make the new place your home for many years to come and become part of the community, or, do you love the adventure of living in many different places while taking advantage of financial opportunities along the way? Many of my friends have upgraded several times, with each move into newer or more luxurious condos taking a step towards building more equity. Yet, they all say that they are happy homeowners—and that is what matters most.

All of these concepts are on the market right now, in an abundance like never before. Before you enter the real estate market, however, it is of utmost importance to prepare yourself and do some research into the new products. This book can help you to get started.

As the old neighbourhood changes and everywhere new construction is booming, the array of possibilities becomes overwhelming. Without much study, many people make far-reaching decisions that will impact their lives in major ways for many years. This user-friendly guide, with its wide collection of basic information, will sharpen your skills in dealing with situations before you get carried away in the excitement of the moment. This book does not claim superior expertise in the field, but aims at addressing the subject of real estate as it comes up for an average buyer or seller in this market. The book provides the basic knowledge you need before you proceed with important decisions, and it passes on some valuable market experience from a selection of local real estate investors and the author herself, making it an extensive source of hands-on information.

The book also provides extensive knowledge you'll need to be financially successful and emotionally happy with your real estate endeavours. Real estate investing can be a profitable and enjoyable enterprise. Chances are that, with the use of bank financing, real estate investments are the biggest and most expensive investments you'll make in your lifetime.

Planning ahead when you buy your first home, buy an investment condo, or downsize for retirement always gives you an advantage. No matter which side you are on—buying or selling—this book will help in your search for a real estate agent or a property manager, help you as you investigate financing and the right mortgage, and help you evaluate risks and buy insurance. I will provide valuable advice on important issues such as when to buy, what to buy, and how to buy. I will explain in great detail financially successful strategies to help you achieve all your real estate investment goals. The book also looks at today's real estate market in Canada where timing and the location of your future real estate investments are more important than ever before.

This book will guide you step by step. It will provide a framework of steps you can take to build home equity. There are choices about how to get there. When you make informed decisions, your route to financial success becomes much safer, allowing for peace of mind and stability. This book is written in a highly readable fashion—for readers who are in the market to buy or sell real estate. If you are interested in a specific issue and read only one chapter at a time, I hope you will find the information helpful. I also hope the theoretical experiences will prepare you to apply your new knowledge when the timing is right. Good luck with all your real estate investments!

PART ONE:

MAKING THE DECISION TO BUY PROPERTY

Chapter 1:

Real Estate and the Economy

Real estate is part of the economy. Over the last several years, Canada has shown strong economic growth from coast to coast, and the real estate market has followed this trend. This economic growth put consumers in a favourable position, and Canada experienced a housing boom. However, as economies can weaken, housing markets can follow suit with a downturn. It is important that you, as an investor, are aware of the cyclical nature of the real estate market. This chapter provides you with insight about how the economy and the real estate market are tied together.

Canada's Housing Boom

Real estate in Canada, especially in the western provinces, has been growing at an astounding pace. Nationwide, and for many years now, values and prices have been rising in all categories of real estate, as this booming housing market is supported by more jobs, low unemployment, fairly low interest rates, and, therefore, low mortgage rates. As a result, condos and housing projects in prime locations often are sold out even before they are built. This kind of market creates its own rules. Developers now try to sell part of the product before construction starts, and the remainder as construction moves along. This enables them to constantly adjust prices to market conditions.

Besides reacting to interest rates and mortgage rates, a market always reacts to what attracts people to an area. The oil boom is attracting people of working age to move to Alberta, and they need housing. Consequently, in Alberta there is a housing shortage, which is what has driven up the real estate prices tremendously. Albertans of retirement age profit from that situation, sell out, and move to British Columbia for their golden years. The mild climate in British Columbia is ideal for seniors, and there they can enjoy such year-round attractions as golfing, fishing, and sailing. The laid-back lifestyle along the scenic coastlines creates a steady inflow of migration into a world away from high traffic, crime, and the competitiveness of the industrialized centers, while new communication systems facilitate family connections over long distances.

Never before has Canada seen such large numbers of well-heeled people retiring at once. Many of the retirees are expected to have another twenty years of meaningful time on their side—a creative golden age. These people are intent on building their future, and their input is rather important and highly visible. City planners and developers try to conceptualize baby boomers' dreams as well as the infrastructure that will be necessary to accommodate this growth. New communities come to life. The affluence of the new retirees can spread among many people. Good concepts draw more and more people, and the system feeds on itself, creating the need for more housing and more services.

Consumer confidence at all age levels has grown by leaps and bounds and is evident all over the country. Ottawa has seen its economy evolve. Where once the province relied on one major employer, it now is driven by a very vibrant high-tech industry, which has had a very strong positive impact on demand for residential housing.

Saskatchewan recently has gained its fair share of economic growth. The recent move by the local economy into the resource sector has boosted the real estate market. Saskatchewan's economy now is thriving on the uranium, potash, and grain markets. In fact, according to a report of the Canadian Real Estate Association on May 31, 2007: "Of all the Western provinces, no where is the real estate market as hot as in Saskatchewan ... Saskatchewan has the largest percentage increase in annual unit sales and new listings of all provinces." [i]

Toronto, and the greater Toronto area (GTA), continue to have a strong and healthy real estate market. Due to immigration, job growth and strong employment numbers in the area, real estate prices in the GTA are still on the rise. There is an abundance of housing choices in the GTA market, which provides the underlying strength of a healthy market. Housing prices in Toronto are relatively high compared to prices in other parts of the country. For example, Toronto's housing prices are higher than those in Calgary and Edmonton, even though the rate at which prices are growing currently is the highest in these two later cities.

Real Estate Cycles

Like many other investment markets, real estate is cyclical in nature. It is as good as impossible to make plans and to correctly predict the exact time of upward and downward movements on a long term scale. The eventual length of a cycle is unpredictable. If your main concern is to own a home and to live in a lovely location, and you find a beautiful place, it might be best to go ahead and buy. If your main concern is to be in the market and to make money with your real estate investments, you might consider a different purchase. From an investment point of view, try to buy and hold in the up cycle. Conversely, get out of the market and take your profit before the down cycle kicks in.

The cyclical nature of real estate is also reflected in the various stages of the market. In real estate, there are what are called sellers' markets and buyers' markets. In a sellers' market there is less supply in the market place; buyers need to be quick in making their buying decisions, as multiple offers on a single property are not uncommon. Also, in a sellers' market we see an increase in the average sales price and number of transactions. After a sellers' market has been in place for a period of time, there is a tendency for the market to balance itself. In a buyers' market there is more product on the market, and buyers take their time when making their purchasing decision. Prices can be negotiated, and sellers often accept offers as they come in.

As is often the case, periods with low interest rates and full employment go hand in hand with up cycles. Periods with high interest rates, high defaults on mortgage payments, and more layoffs than new job opportunities are often associated with down cycles. The smart home buyer/investor correlates his investing with these market cycles for the best long-term asset management. Yet, it is very difficult to nail down the tops and bottoms of these cycles as they happen. Often we manage to track them accurately only in hindsight analysis.

Yet consumer sentiment is not only dependent on interest rates and job growth, which are internal factors of the economy. Another factor that influences Canadian market conditions is world markets. A possible downturn in the Canadian market could happen if the slowdown of the U.S. economy were to affect Canada and have a negative impact on the Canadian economy, as 85 per cent of Canada's trade is with the United States. As a spill-over effect of a slowdown in the U.S. economy, we could see less job growth and higher unemployment in Canada, which would ultimately dampen the surge in the Canadian housing market. For example, due to the decline of housing starts associated with the U.S. home slump, British Columbia's softwood lumber export industry plunged 24 per cent in the first quarter of 2007.

Also to consider is the current value of the Canadian dollar. According to CIBC World Markets (an arm of the Canadian Imperial Bank of Commerce), in a statement made June 1, 2007: "The Canadian dollar will reach parity with the U.S. currency by the end of 2007 with the help of high commodity prices, ongoing merger-related interest and higher interest rates."[ii]

As the Canadian dollar continues to gain strength against the U.S. dollar, Canada's exports become more and more expensive for U.S. importers. The higher currency not only reduces profit margins, but could ultimately lead to a decline in demand for Canadian exports by the United States and, consequently, we could see more job losses in the manufacturing industry in Canada. And, people who lose their jobs don't buy homes. Even Canada's flourishing resources industry, with exports going as far away as China and India, would lose some of its competitive advantage with the rising Canadian dollar.

In a country as large and diverse as Canada, the real estate market is also determined by local economies. Housing markets are specific to the different regions of the country and reflect the prosperity of the local economies. Economic growth figures in Alberta and British Columbia were ahead of the national average in 2006; among economists, the prediction was that this trend would continue in 2007. The strong housing growth in Alberta is based on the worldwide strong commodities boom; specifically, oil and gas. Residents of Alberta who work in the oil and gas sector have high incomes and can afford to pay for new housing, with new home prices in Calgary up a whopping 61 per cent from October 2005 to October 2006, and home prices in Edmonton up by 38 per cent in the same time period, according to Statistics Canada.[iii]

British Columbia's housing boom reflects a surge in positive migration brought about by British Columbia's mild climate and exceptional recreational facilities. However, on the other hand, real estate markets in Ontario, Quebec, and the Atlantic Canada provinces have cooled off since 2004. These later markets have seen only single-digit growth in housing prices and it looks like these provinces are experiencing a soft landing.

After real estate markets have had a spectacular climb nationwide in the 11 per cent range in just one year (MLS national average home and property price[iv]: June 2007, $315,332; June 2006, $283,655), according to statistics compiled by the Canadian Real Estate Association, investors are well advised to take notice that this may be an unsustainable growth rate.

Such growth may be balanced with lower single-digit growth in coming years. These housing price increases, in combination with possible higher interest rates in the future, will eventually make housing less affordable, and, consequently, housing demand may soften and level off. Especially in cities such as Calgary, Edmonton, and Vancouver, some economists warn that the spectacular run-up in prices may flatten out or even pull back in the future. It would be a dangerous assumption that real estate investments could be used like ATM machines with financial institutions continuously lending more money year after year, guaranteed by a stellar increase of value by your equity. This is elusive thinking. It is at your own peril that you forget that the market runs in cycles. In a down-cycle homeowners could be struggling just to keep their homes, never mind taking out more money against their homes.

Table 1.1 Average MLS Home and Property Prices per Province

Province	June 2007	June 2006	Per cent change
British Columbia	$446,893	$399,829	11.8%
Alberta	$364,072	$291,843	24.7%
Saskatchewan	$180,934	$134,161	34.9%
Manitoba	$179,531	$155,531	15.4%
Ontario	$304,699	$280,208	8.7%
Quebec	$211,206	$198,462	6.4%
New Brunswick	$142,734	$127,406	12.0%
Prince Edward Island	$134,295	$134,115	.1%
Nova Scotia	$191,593	$170,607	12.3%
Newfoundland	$152,641	$132,571	15.1%
Northwest Territories	$314,022	$243,745	28.8%
Yukon	$209,687	$177,191	18.1%
Nation	$315,332	$283,655	11.2%

SOURCE: CREA Canadian Real Estate Association[v]

House prices across Canada have reached new record highs. Average prices in June 2007 hit new monthly records in Alberta, Saskatchewan, Ontario, New Brunswick, Nova Scotia, Newfoundland, and Labrador. Sales activity set new quarterly records in the following provinces: Alberta, Saskatchewan, Manitoba, Ontario, Quebec, New Brunswick, and Nova Scotia.

With the historic record of double-digit percentage gains in real estate values over the past years, we need to keep in mind that chances are that the housing market could level off or even retreat. History shows that no market goes only up and up and up. A market correction must be expected at some time. However, no one holds the crystal ball that can predict with certainty if and when this might happen. When people are looking to buy a home for themselves and a good opportunity presents itself, generally speaking, they should go ahead and buy. Once an ideal place is sold to another buyer, that genuine opportunity might not come up again for some time. However, when assessing the financial risks in a hot market, it is wise not to allow yourself to be financially stretched to the limit. It is essential to set aside funds for the unforeseen: unexpected maintenance and repair expenses, special assessments for properties that form part of a strata, higher assessment notices over time in residential taxation, or higher interest rates and therefore higher mortgage or credit line payments.

Though one cannot successfully predict a market peak ahead of time, there are parameters that are fairly indicative of the changes ahead. Follow the newspapers closely for a number of monthly statistics available, and check the statistics published regularly by the local real estate board. Real estate boards provide an opinion on market conditions and these reports are made public.

There are, amongst others, three indicators that could predict a cooling-off period in the housing market:

1. The first indication is widespread price reductions. They usually occur when properties are harder to sell and the "for sale" signs have been out for an extended period of time.

2. Once a good real estate market has prevailed for an extended period time, builders become encouraged and a lot of new product comes on the market. This creates an imbalance between supply and demand, and eventually could lead to a levelling off or even a decline in prices. However, if the housing starts are embraced enthusiastically by the market, and inventory of new housing available remains low, as is the case in a housing boom, prices may still go up. A change in the situation for sure will be initiated when the Bank of Canada becomes worried about inflation and stops the building boom by raising interest rates, with higher mortgage rates following suit.

3. The number of applications for new mortgages declines significantly. Again, this statistic is made available to the public.

Market timing is always a risky business. No one is able to predict the future with certainty. Not only is it difficult to time the market, but the evaluation of risk factors and personal strategies depends on the psychological profile of the players in the market. Some investors may judge the market to be at the top and therefore keep out of the market, consequently possibly missing a good housing rally and maybe having a financial setback when entering the market at a later time. In this regard, for those selling out for profit it may be inconceivable that others are buying in order to grab opportunities before ownership becomes unaffordable. But this is exactly the nature of the market. On the other end, during a downturn in the housing market, the investor may think the market has declined as far as it will. He will buy, yet the possibility remains that the market may decline even further.

The obvious conclusion to this dilemma is to stay invested within a safe margin at all times. As the best of minds have difficulties in timing the market correctly, it might be wise for you, as an investor, to hold on to some assets while divesting yourself of others to minimize risk and to cash in on profits before they diminish. Focus on the good deals out there and step away from the bad investments. As with any other asset class, the level of exposure and your overall debt-to-equity ratio should be sensible and should vary with market conditions. Always maintain a sufficient cash basis to bring you through the downward cycle of the real estate market and enable you to have the time and patience to wait until the market turns around and new opportunities become available.

The most obvious goal with rental properties is positive cash flow, although you could consider a purchase that would provide negative cash flow if it is a great value to buy and there seems to be the possibility of reselling in the short term with considerable profit. When your rental property has a positive cash flow you can sit out any negative turn in the cycle and, as a smart investor, consider cashing in when the cycle is on top.

After each downswing there will be another upturn in the market. However, you have to decide if an exit from the market will be cost efficient. As always, when buying and selling, take into consideration related expenses and capital gains tax and income tax.

Protecting Yourself against a Market Downturn

What happens when the market turns down? As a prudent investor, you must expect a housing market downturn at some point in your real estate investing career. Can you take measures to prevent falling down with it? Yes, you can. The most important thing you can do to protect yourself is to use only a reasonable amount of leverage. Here is how it works: The bank lends you an amount of money in the form of a credit line or a mortgage based on the assessed value of your property. The assessed value may have been determined by your bank's appraiser. Should the housing market decline significantly, the bank will have the value of your property reassessed. As the bank has agreed to lend you a fixed percentage of the assessed value of your property, when that value drops significantly, the bank may require you to come up with additional money. If you cannot make this additional payment, you may be forced to sell the property. By the time you sell, real estate prices have dropped and the profit on your investment will have shrunk. You may even incur a loss if the sale price turns out to be lower than the initial purchase price. Even worse, other investors are in the same bad spot, so everybody is selling into a deteriorating market. A glut of product will send prices tumbling even further.

To protect yourself against a market downturn, it is good advice to:

- *Avoid no–down payment loans.* With this type of loan, with the slightest drop in market prices, the bank or lender will request an additional payment to maintain the loan-to-value ratio. If you do not want to postpone your purchase, and you cannot come up with the down payment, make sure you have a secure job with a steady monthly income as a financial backup before you take out a no–down payment loan.

- *Never take as much money as your lender is willing to offer you.* Play it safe in the event of a real estate downturn by keeping your borrowed amount below the percentage of assessed value figure the bank is willing to loan you. Consider a less-pricey investment to meet this objective. There are a few variables to play with; for example, start small and upgrade later. Or, consider a neighbourhood that is not as pricey as the "in vogue" neighbourhoods.

- *Always maintain a large enough safety margin.* As the value of your home or other real estate investments rises, avoid refinancing to the maximum; in other words, avoid taking out all the equity for other use, such as for home renovations, a new car, a holiday, or even to purchase another investment property.

- *Use leverage to your advantage.* The astute investor must have a clear concept in terms of leverage: the leverage one achieves when working with credit—be it a mortgage, a credit line, or private financing—is favourable when markets rise and can be detrimental when markets fall.
   Let us look at examples of leverage, both in a rising market and in a falling market. For the sake of simplicity, let's do this without taking into consideration expenses such as insurance, property taxes, interest payments, and closing costs. In the example below we are assuming that the market value of the home appreciated/depreciated by $30,000—10 per cent of the initial purchase price. Due to leverage, however, as you can

see in Table 1.2, with the sale of the investment, the gain/loss is 40 per cent positive in a rising market and 40 per cent negative in a falling market. In a rising market, home ownership can provide a significant return on the initial investment; in a falling market the opposite is true, and home ownership can lead to losses.

Table 1.2 Leverage on Your Investment

	Rising market	Falling market
Purchase price	$300,000	$300,000
Down payment (25 per cent)	$75,000	$75,000
Credit line	$225,000	$225,000
Appreciation/depreciation	10 per cent	(10 per cent)
Sale price	$330,000	$270,000
Pay-back credit line	$225,000	$225,000
Cash left	$105,000	$45,000
Return on investment	140 per cent	60 per cent
Gain/loss	40 per cent	(40 per cent)

There is reason to be cautious. The Bank of Canada has its inflation target pegged around the 2 per cent level. When rates move above this level, the bank sees a need to protect consumers from rising inflation and will initiate counteractive measures. The second quarter of 2007 has given mixed signals: The high Canadian dollar has had a dampening effect on exports, which correlates with Canadian job losses in the export industry. Yet, in the same period, energy prices have been steadily rising, which has lead to slight inflationary pressures. According to the Centre for Global Energy Studies, "As long as capacity remains inadequate to meet gasoline demand and OPEC responds by restricting output to keep prices too high, the oil market's current period of high and volatile prices will continue."[vi]

On the other hand, if a global slowdown were to emerge, energy prices could go lower rather than higher.

Let us look at the case of rising interest rates in Canada in the early 1980s. This replay of the 1980s should in no way be interpreted as a prediction. It is just a demonstration of what can happen when interest rates rise. It should give you a feeling for how markets work and how a downturn affects everybody. In 1981, as the Bank of Canada increased interest rates from 7.5 per cent to 21 per cent to match the monetary policy of the United States, the real estate market in all of Canada fell sharply, region by region. At the time, the U.S. Federal Reserve was attempting, through its monetary policies, to counteract the inflation brought about by the very high price of oil. In 1981, home owners who had little equity tied up in their homes, but who were rather leveraged out to the maximum, were forced to give up their homes as they were in no position to meet the high mortgage payments. Banks took over these abandoned homes, there were more and more homes up for sale, and housing prices took a nosedive.

An illustration of the stagnant real estate market in the 1980s, and what happened to some investors, is given in Christa's story:

Christa's Story

Christa bought a fixer-upper older house in a downtown neighbourhood of a small town. Christa's boyfriend was an architect by profession, and together they redesigned and renovated the entire house. He had the expertise and the time to do so.

However, in the early 1980s, after they purchased the house, house prices fell steeply. The house could no longer be sold with a profit. In order not to incur a loss, Christa decided to rent out the house for a few years. Unfortunately, the tenants turned out not to be the greatest, and the house needed to be renovated and repaired over and over again. One tenant disappeared without notice and simply left the keys under the doormat and a note on the kitchen counter. Soon Christa was fed up and decided to hire a property management firm to manage her rental property. However, neither the necessary upkeep of the house nor the overall market situation improved.

After seven years of renting out the house, Christa decided to sell. There was no chance of a profit despite the amount of work that had been put into the house: as unbelievable as it may sound, even after seven years and all the redesigning and renovation, her selling price was the same as her initial purchase price.

At the time of her purchase, Christa had been a novice investor with no knowledge of the cyclical nature of markets. She had inherited some money, which she had put into her own house project. But, because of the stagnant real estate market, she could have fared much better by just investing the money in a guaranteed investment certificate (GIC).

Over time the real estate market rotated again and interest rates came down considerably. If Christa only had held on to the property a little longer she could have sold it for a nice profit.

Learn from this story: Inevitably, Christa lost her patience with her investment in her house and decided to sell during a market downturn, foregoing all the profit she could have made if she waited for the real estate market to pick up again. The lesson to be learned here is that, with any investment, be it real estate or an investment in another asset class, sometimes you need to take a very long breath and hold on to your investment until the market turns around and reaches a new top. Resist the temptation to liquidate your investment too early because you are fed up with the investment or you are not seeing the profit you expected to see. This "game" can be a real science. Waiting out a down cycle in real estate can take many years, but, in the end, patience will pay off.

Conclusion

A solid economy with low unemployment, good job growth, and low inflation supports a strong housing market. However, as economic growth is regional and cyclical, the real estate market is also regional and cyclical. The current housing boom in different regions of Canada may one day come to an end if and when employment falls, inflation rises, and interest rates—and therefore mortgage rates—rise. No one can predict when this may happen. Therefore, learn to manage risk when making real estate investments: avoid refinancing your home and other properties to the maximum, avoid no–down payment loans, invest moderately, and always keep emergency cash on hand.

> ### Key Points
>
> ❖ Use leverage in moderation so you don't lose your home in a downturn.
> ❖ Know there are cycles. Be aware of the direction of the current cycle.
> ❖ Stay invested moderately at all times.
> ❖ Invest in good deals.
> ❖ Always have a comfortable safety margin.
> ❖ Never take as much money as your lender is willing to offer you.

Chapter 2:

Personal Finances

Your main investment goal should be financial security; in other words, managing your risk, and making money with your investments—the more the better. You also want to have a portfolio of assets that protects against inflation; remember, a dollar tomorrow is worth less than a dollar today. By investing in your own home or in an investment property and, at the same time, diversifying among other financial assets as well, you can achieve these financial goals. However, you yourself have to decide when the time is right to purchase your real estate assets.

A budget is the first step in achieving financial security and properly managing financial risks. It can sometimes be quite a challenge to stay within pre-set budget limits when you are investing in real estate. To format your budget, estimate and include all potential costs—present and future—associated with a real estate purchase. If the project you have your sights set on does not completely match your budget, there are "mortgage helpers." All these considerations will be explained in detail on the following pages.

Allocating Your Assets

The number one rule in asset allocation is to diversify. Real estate is one of the best ways to protect yourself against inflation, but you have to make sure that you also protect yourself against a possible downturn in the real estate market. There is an old saying that has a lot of truth to it: "Don't put all your eggs into one basket." It generally is a good idea to diversify investments among different asset classes such as cash, Guaranteed Investment Certificates (GCIs), mutual funds, bonds, stocks, natural resources, international investments, and other investment vehicles such as Registered Retirement Savings Plans (RRSPs), annuities, and, of course, real estate. If one asset class goes out of fashion, another will most likely go the opposite way and appreciate. The market of investments essentially rotates. If you diversify among the different asset classes, the overall volatility of your assets will be diminished and the total return on all investments together will improve.

Where is best place to invest your hard-earned money? One of the smartest answers could be: at the right time, in your own home. Instead of monthly rent payments, you will make regular mortgage or credit line payments, which translate into automatic savings and the building of your own nest egg. As you build equity over time, living in your own home will provide you with emotional and financial security—even at the point of retirement when you can use your home for a reverse mortgage. Moreover, when the value of your home appreciates over the years, and for any reason you consider selling your home, the appreciation that occurred will be tax exempt, for this was your principal residence. The taxation of true rental investment properties (not properties to be bought and flipped in a short time frame) in Canada is also favourable. In the case of the sale of a rental property, the ensuing capital gain is only 50 per cent taxable. Should you have incurred capital losses in other years, even in areas such as stock or mutual fund trading, your capital gains made in real estate trading can be offset with these capital losses, resulting in you paying less tax.

Over the last few years people have become wary of investing only in "paper." There seems to be a trend back to investing in tangible hard assets. Although we are told that inflation is under control, most people are shocked when they go to buy a car, a building lot, or a house and they compare prices to those of ten or twenty years ago. Jobs are no longer guaranteed for a lifetime to provide us with steady income. Life expectancy is steadily rising; there needs to be a balance so that we have funds to draw on as we age. So, it makes a lot of sense that people try to secure their standard of living by holding on to hard assets. High demand for all the various forms of property leads to rising prices in this asset class. Of course, the low unemployment and the low interest rates and, therefore, the low mortgage rates equally stimulate demand, as under such favourable conditions real estate currently becomes affordable for many people.

Real estate is a natural hedge against inflation. As inflation rises, real estate prices also rise. The same cannot be said, for example, of bond investments. Bonds offer no hedge against inflation. If you buy a ten-year bond for a certain amount of money close to par, and live off the interest of that bond, at the maturity of the bond you will receive back the same amount you invested earlier. In contrast to this, the value of real estate rises with inflation. When you sell your property after having held on to it for many years, generally the money you get is more than the initial investment.

As the previous chapter explained, real estate markets run in cycles. If you buy at the bottom of the cycle and sell at the top, you can cash in solid profits. If, on the other hand, you buy at the top and sell at the bottom, your profit potential will not be maximized. You could incur a loss. If you get everything right and invest in real estate when the cycle has momentum to the upside, the idea of diversification again seems to be prudent. This means that you refinance and take some of the equity out of your home and/or other real estate investment properties. You can then reinvest this cash can into RRSPs, mutual funds, GICs, stocks, or bonds etc. As an investor, you thus experience broader exposure to various market conditions. As the various markets rarely move in tandem, the risks are spread more evenly.

If you desire to play the real estate market in a different way from investing in properties yourself, you can achieve this with Real Estate Investment Trusts (REITs). With this kind of investment, you do not buy the actual real estate with all the problems of financing, renting out, and insuring the property and thus avoid dealing with real estate agents, lawyers, and the associated costs. An equity REIT invests in a portfolio of real estate properties. REITs trade on the stock exchange and can easily be bought or sold. Such trading ensures liquidity of your money, yet is not for the faint of heart. As with stocks, there are ups and downs, a phenomenon the professionals call "volatility." REITs pay out dividends generated by the rental income of the portfolio of rental properties of a particular REIT. So you can tie the performance of your funds to the real estate success story of large pools of money. Of course, that performance then is also subject to the appreciation of the properties that make up the fund's investments.

Another way to diversify your real estate investment portfolio is by investing in stocks or mutual funds that hold real estate. Ask your mutual fund broker for the track record of real estate mutual funds that have been on the Canadian market for several years in order to choose the best among them. In the same line of thinking, if you should become interested in real estate related stocks, analyze their recent performance, plotted through graphs, as well as current information on the sector, to be able to make an informed purchase decision.

In summary, to reduce the risks associated with the cyclical nature of real estate, as a prudent investor, diversify your assets into various asset classes, and strive to diversify within the real estate category. After building equity for an extended period of time, make sure that not all your money is invested in just one particular asset class. For example, if your principle residence were your only investment, you may want to look at refinancing your home; in other words, take out some of the equity, and invest it in another asset class such as bonds, GICs, treasury bills, stocks, or mutual funds. Here again, the right timing in making these changes also plays an important role. To diversify within your real estate portfolio, if you own your principle residence in one location, consider an investment property in another location (real estate could gain strength in one neigh-bourhood, town, city, or even province, while lagging behind in other areas). If you are an investor in stocks and mutual funds, consider adding real estate–related securities to your portfolio.

Should I Rent or Should I Buy?

With home ownership, it is obvious and common knowledge that you no longer pay rent, but rather pay down a mortgage and build up equity. The important question of when to buy and when to rent is less obvious, yet could contribute to building wealth more than you think.

When is it smarter to buy?

There are circumstances when it is smarter to buy a house than to rent one. The following is a list of conditions that favour buying a home:

- *Year after year the home appreciates in value.* When you work with a real estate agent, he or she may tell you that there is statistical evidence of an average historical appreciation of about 5 per cent on an annual basis over the past twenty-five years for the average Canadian home. However, according to an analysis done by RE/MAX, in the top ten real estate markets across the country, statistics point to an even greater apprecia-tion of 8 per cent on an annual basis for the past twenty-five years. This long-term gain is essential to building equity. It could be the most important factor to creating wealth for many people.

  According to research and statistical material compiled by RE/MAX and published by the *Times Colonist*, Victoria, Vancouver Island, in the January 25, 2007 edition, the following table shows the astonishing growth rates of the residential average prices of all types of housing of various Canadian cities between 1981 and 2006:

Table 2.1 Residential MLS Average Price. All Types of Housing.[vii]

Market	1981	2006	Per cent change
Vancouver	$148,861	$509,876	242%
Victoria	$121,648	$400,000	229%
Kelowna	$104,285	$323,978	211%
Calgary	$106,033	$346,673	227%
Edmonton	$91,438	$250,915	174%
Regina	$54,915	$131,851	140%
Saskatoon	$64,756	$160,577	148%
Winnipeg	$52,656	$151,983	189%
London	$57,989	$190,521	228%
St. Catherines	$49,655	$213,032	329%
Hamilton-Burlington	$58,508	$248,400	325%
Toronto	$90,203	$351,941	290%
Barrie	$51,665	$244,000	372%
Ottawa	$64,854	$257,481	297%
Montreal	$55,004	$215,659	292%
Halifax-Dartmouth	$59,366	$203,178	242%
Moncton	$44,338	$130,000	193%
St.John's	$55,067	$139,300	153%
National	$76,021	$276,824	264%

SOURCE: CREA,TREB,OMREB,CREB,EREB,REMAX

Yet, the past does not always indicate what the future will bring. In addition, markets are not only cyclical, but also more and more influenced by global developments.

• *A mortgage acts like a savings plan.* With regular mortgage payments, you are basically forced to put a certain amount of money aside each payment period and, at the same time, you build equity.

• *A credit line allows you to take out credit at a low interest rate any time you need it up to the limit established.* If you finance the purchase of your home with a credit line and pay only the interest on the credit line, the increased value of your home year by year through appreciation will still be saved. Although credit lines leave you vulnerable to changes in interest rates, they allow you down payments without penalties whenever you have a chance to do so. If unexpected expenses come your way, the full line of credit is at your disposal again—no need for that extra rainy day fund.

- *The current state of the market is a challenge.* With the current situation in the housing market, it can be quite a challenge to find a home you like and can afford. Buying a home or an investment property has never been this expensive before. According to an article published by Can West News Service in the *Times Colonist* on September 20, 2006, written by Eric Beauchesne, "The dream of home ownership is becoming just that, a dream, for more and more Canadians as rising prices and interest rates outpace growth in incomes and erode the affordability of homes, especially in Western Canada."[viii]

  With soaring prices in cities such as Vancouver, Victoria, Toronto, and Montreal, people require more and more pre-tax income to be able to afford the mortgage payments and property taxes on a home. Across the country, the most affordable type of home is still a condominium. Next is a townhouse, then a detached bungalow, and, finally, the least affordable home is a two-storey home. The question arises, is it still smarter to buy than rent? One point to keep in mind is that, when housing prices rise because of soaring construction costs, the rents will follow suit.

- *Lower interest rates and more attractive financing options make home-ownership possible.* Historically low interest rates, and therefore lower mortgage or credit line payments, and a whole new array of financing options (for example, mortgages with extended amortization periods up to forty years) are making homeownership more affordable for the average Canadian household.

- *Homeownership provides a feeling of security.* Owning your own home gives you peace of mind and the freedom to do with your home whatever you want, as long as you abide by the local bylaws. If you plan to live in your own home for a long time, that home most likely gives you the feelings of security and safety.

- *Homeownership is a hedge against inflation.* Though markets are cyclical, Canada has had the annual inflation rate targeted at 2 per cent for some time now, which translates into 20 per cent inflation over a period of ten years. The experience over the last few years shows real estate appreciating well above these figures, even when comparing statistics for regional diversity. For all of Canada, as of January 2007, a survey done by RE/MAX, a nationwide leading real estate agency, put the figures for the residential Multiple Listing Service (MLS) prices over the last twenty-five years up a whopping 264 per cent (11 per cent annually). The report also pinpointed that a major factor for this growth was the 25 per cent increase in Canada's population over this time period.[ix]

Various other statistics are available on the Internet. This means it might be a good idea to invest in a condo for you or your parents as part of a retirement plan to balance fixed income instruments like GICs or government bonds. Or, think about your teenagers, who are soon to enter university. Instead of renting, they could share a condo. If the pace of real estate appreciation continues for years to come, this could be a viable option and a smart way to pay for evermore expensive education.

When Is it Smarter to Rent?

Though in the long run prices will move higher, there could be a short-term correction, or prices could level off for a while. There are people analyzing this hot market with a lot of scepticism. If you come to the conclusion that the lofty prices have created a bubble and these prices are unsustainable, logic would then demand a different strategy. The approach would be to lock in profits and exit the market until there is another point for re-entry at potentially lower prices. The advantages of renting could be:

- *Save up a down payment.* Rent while you save money for a down payment. Look into home ownership when conditions are favourable.

- *Renting can provide less worry for professional career and family matters.* An important factor in deciding whether to buy a home or to rent is your outlook on your professional career, your family interests, and the necessities dictated by your life circumstances. You need to ask yourself if you can settle down at a given location for several years. If this question can be answered affirmatively, you don't really have to worry so much about the ups and downs of market direction, and this will eliminate a lot of anxiety if the market swings one way or the other.

    Once you have decided that you want to own your place, there is a whole list of expenses to consider: it will cost you to hire a moving company, it will cost you to buy the property, it will cost you to sell the property, and it will cost you to maintain the property while you live in it. And then you have to add property taxes on top of that. An established trend in the housing market might change and run in the opposite direction. Are you prepared to take this risk? What if your professional career forces you to be open to relocation? You then might not be able to ride out a negative cycle and stay financially ahead when adding up all the costs involved when moving close to that future employment location. This could mean that, under current conditions, your purchase price, including all related expenses, would be higher than the money you reasonably can expect to receive when you try to sell after owning for only a short time. The search for a suitable home may not be worth it when you already know that in a short time you have to move on.

• *Renting is a consideration for seniors.* Seniors may consider renting after they sell their homes and before they relocate. If you are well advanced in the life cycle, a red-hot market allows a good downsizing strategy. You could sell the large old family homestead and rent for a while until you find a nice condo that is easy to keep up. Or, you could try to find a property located close to where your children live. If you are burdened with health problems, you could move closer to a good hospital. Downsizing might be desirable for a variety of reasons and generally provides you with additional cash for retirement.

Deciding on Your Budget

So how do you know what you can afford? What you can afford is determined through a balance of your income with your obligations. Then you can begin a wish list. Do you want to buy your first house, first condo, or first rental property? Follow these steps to establish your budget.

1. **Ask the lender.** The bank, the mortgage broker, or the lender will have the property appraised. They will offer you various options and fee structures from which to choose. You will receive a financial framework that shows how much credit is available considering the project and your personal income and financial situation. Here the budgeting process will start: Can you afford a down payment? How much of a down payment can you manage? Further, how much of your monthly income can you afford to set aside for the mortgage payments, for interest payments on

credit lines, for strata fees, property taxes, insurance, etc? Or, in the case of an investment, the questions may be: When do you achieve positive cash flow? Will the project be feasible?

2. ***Decide on your own personal limits for borrowing.*** Regardless of how much money your lender is willing to lend to you, you have to feel comfortable with the overall financial picture. The institution, be it your bank or mortgage broker, tells you what is affordable for you from the viewpoint of their own lending guidelines. You still have to balance this with a personal notion of security and a willingness to commit to setting these goals. This means you choose from available options, and then establish your own personal financial framework. Effectively, you then should set your own limits for borrowing. You know what other expenses and financial commitments you may have. Also, you have a feeling for how much debt you would be comfortable carrying, now or in the future. In other words, only you know your risk tolerance. Therefore it is your responsibility to make the final decision on which loan is right. After signing a contract involving real estate, you cannot change your mind all that easily. It is much wiser to budget first and then stay within those financial limits. So, affordability not only depends on the banker's offer, but also on personal needs. Ask yourself and be very honest about it: what would the bottom line of your total debt look like? If you are considering buying an investment in addition to your own home, you need to know the percentage of debt to the fair market value of your other real estate assets or to the total of your assets. After all, you want to enjoy your investment—and be able to sleep at night.

3. ***Avoid any hasty decisions.*** It is a smart idea to have pre-approved financing in place before you look at properties. This ensures that you will not get carried away in today's fast-paced bidding process. There is a lot of weight behind an offer on the table that comes with pre-approved financing. With this measure in place, you will not overextend yourself financially, thus enabling you to hold on to the property you purchase for as long as you wish. Don't forget, if interest rates were to rise significantly, your regular mortgage or credit line payments would jump as well. With a careful budgeting process, you can easily outmanoeuver any market downturn, and, most of the time, will find suitable conditions to refinance when markets and interest rates change.

4. *Calculate additional costs.* Would you like to upgrade and renovate your new home? The cost of new cabinets, new appliances, new countertops, and new flooring must all be included as part of your budget. Or, does your new home need extensive repairs and maintenance to make it liveable? Does your new home need a new roof in the near future? Or, does your community plan to hook your property on to the public sewage system and is going to charge you thousands of dollars in hook-up fees? If so, you need to budget these costs.

5. *Budget for rising interest rates.* Unless you have taken out a fixed-rate mortgage, any increase in interest rates by the central bank would translate into higher mortgage or credit line payments for you. Although rising interest rates are an uncertainty, you nevertheless have to foolproof your budget in every possible way.

6. *Expect vacancies of your rental properties.* Although today's hot real estate market goes hand in hand with low vacancy rates, be prepared for a vacancy of a month or two—especially when you have a substantial tenant turnover rate or you have to look for new tenants in the winter. Chances are that you might not only miss out on the occasional rent payments but, to fill vacancies, you will have the additional costs of advertising, cleaning, painting, etc. If all this takes away too much of your precious time and you then decide to have the property taken care of by a property management firm, it is good to know that these agencies charge close to 10 per cent of the rent—and this arrangement does not guarantee a zero vacancy rate. You have to be knowledgeable about the going rate of leases and base your budget on the correct amount. As an example, by lowering the rent by $100 per month, or approximately 10 per cent of your original asking price, the number of tenants interested in your rental might increase dramatically. This could avoid a prolonged vacancy during winter months when few people consider moving.

7. *Know about special assessments and increasing strata fees.* With a condominium, townhouse, or house on a strata property, there is always the possibility of special assessments and/or significant increases in strata fees. If the budget of the strata has a cost overrun (in other words, the income of the strata does not cover the monetary outlays and expenses) the strata can vote on and approve these extra fees for the owners. Once approved, the special assessments and increased strata fees take effect

immediately and the owner must come up with the funds without delay. These additional costs are not optional. They come out of the blue in the form of elevators that stop functioning, hot water tanks that need immediate replacement, or drainage pipe damage that must be fixed immediately. Contingency funds are not always available, yet repairs cannot be delayed.

8. *Prepare yourself for property tax increases.* Property taxes can jump significantly from one taxation year to the next, as the government annually reassesses the value of your properties to take into consideration skyrocketing property market values.

Finding a Home that Fits into Your Budget

According to a study done by GfK Roper Public Affairs and Media from June 20–27, 2007, most homeowners do not know the actual cost of the mortgage they are paying on. The study found that only one in five homeowners knows what his or her home will ultimately cost, taking into consideration all interest payments on the mortgage throughout its period of amortization. Payments of interest add 150 to 200 per cent of the original loan amount over a twenty-five-year mortgage. In fact, the study shows that 45 per cent of Canadians underestimate the life-time cost of a mortgage. [x]

Learn from the findings of this study: if you plan to hold on to your property for many years to come, ask your banker what the life-time cost of the mortgage on the property will be. Only then will you be able to budget accordingly.

Again, it is important to budget *all* expenses. There are substantial costs associated with owning a home. Rent payments are replaced with regular mortgage payments or interest payments on a credit line; in addition, you'll need to pay home-owner insurance premiums, strata fees if you own a property on a strata, and hefty property taxes. Once a year, city hall will send an assessment notice informing you how much your property tax is. Principle residences qualify for the homeowner's grant or additional deductions if you are over sixty-five. Investment properties or second residences like cottages and timeshares don't qualify and you have to pay the tax in full.

It is optional how much you budget for emergencies, but you must have emergency funds. The roof could start to leak, the hot water tank could explode, the plumbing could need maintenance, etc. It does not matter if you are a home owner or an investor. As an investor, always be vigilant to achieve enough positive cash flow and to have funds set aside so you can avoid being forced to liquidate assets under unfavourable conditions. It is not uncommon for an investor who holds a portfolio of properties with significant equity to be forced to liquidate a property due to insufficient overall cash flow!

People's life situations are as varied as the places they want to live. Mostly it is the budget that limits what is affordable, but the family situation might direct your interest towards a condo, a rancher, a duplex, a townhouse, a multi-level house, or even a farmhouse. The farther away properties are from city centers, the more affordable prices become. For one experienced in remodelling, a duplex or fixer-upper could pave the way to financial success.

More important than the direction a condo or house faces, or even the size of the condo or the house, is the neighbourhood. It is important to find a housing community or strata building where you fit in and feel at ease. This is most essential for your wellbeing. If your budget restrains you in this regard, it is better to wait until you have sufficient funds to settle in a neighbourhood of your liking. Look in areas where development is still in its infancy—generally, these projects are more affordable.

Finding Mortgage Helpers

If, as a first-time home buyer, you set your sights on a property that does not really fit your budget, you can try to find mortgage helpers.

Consider renting out part of your house. Perhaps there is a spare room you can lease to a student. The student's rent could contribute to your mortgage payments and, unless the rent is all inclusive, you could also share the cost of hydro bills, the cost for a basic phone line, and the cost for high-speed Internet connection.

Or, is there a basement in the house that could be transformed into an in-law suite? However, in this case, do check with the local city bylaws on the status of illegal suites to make sure you comply with the city regulations.

Or, if after all, you are not going to need all the space in the house for yourself and your family, would you feel comfortable renting out the upper or lower level of your home?

Will the seller carry part of the debt? Usually in a market downturn, a seller may be desperate enough that he will sell you his property and allow you, for part of the purchase price, to establish a mortgage in his name—or he may offer you financing. In this case, it is not the bank who is your lender, but the seller. Also, the terms of that mortgage are negotiable in your favour and are generally more generous than a mortgage with a bank. The seller allows you this kind of arrangement to facilitate the sale and see it go through.

Consider a Partnership. The big advantage of entering into a partnership when buying real estate is that you can share the costs of your investment with others. What you previously could not afford on your own, now all of the sudden becomes affordable.

To get started, you might opt for a partnership with friends or family or a like-minded investor.

As a note of caution, to stand up in court, investment partnership agreements need to be in writing and need to disclose the rights and responsibilities of each partner in a given timeframe. Once agreements of this nature are signed, they need to be transferred into legal contracts. This is the time to see your lawyer. For example, with a certain project your lawyer will document the percentages of ownership each partner has. A business plan should be in place to allocate profit and losses accordingly. In addition, a risk management plan, together with a timeline for an eventual sale or expansion of the investment, should be worked out. All in all, you need to have guidelines in place that all partners agree on to avoid costly and time-consuming arguments down the road. (A partnership between two partners where each one owns 50 per cent may work better than a partnership where one partner owns 60 per cent and the other partner only owns 40 per cent).

However, even a very subtle and cautious approach does not warrant 100 per cent satisfaction with the execution of your business plan. Not all events and possibilities can be foreseen in advance and, therefore, be put in writing. Even with a written partnership agreement in place, heavy disputes between the partners may arise which may be very difficult to resolve, even in court. A partner may not have been able to fulfill his or her responsibilities for financial or personal reasons.

Partnerships can vary a great deal and there are many different manifestations. Each step in such an innovative partnership must be documented properly. For example, you could have an agreement in which you arrange to buy a fixer-upper with your partner. You would be responsible for the down payment and financing of the project, while your partner would look after the actual renovation project, including both the materials and the work. Once the project is finished, it could be sold, and the profit could be split fifty-fifty.

An example of a very straight forward partnership would be three individuals purchasing an apartment building. They each pay a third of the down payment and then they each take out a mortgage on a third of the remainder of the cost.

Subsequently, they each pay a third of any expenses, such as mortgage payments, insurance payments, property taxes, repairs and renovations. Ultimately they each receive a third of any income, such as rent payments from tenants. If, subsequently, one person wants to sell his share of the house, the other two have the option of buying him out or finding a new third partner. If all three decide to sell the house, each partner would receive a third of the sale price and, therefore, a one-third share in any profit.

Sometimes people with different sets of skills make exceptionally good business partners. Consider one person who has great financial skills and expertise in property management and another person who might be a real estate agent and who has an eye for exceptionally good deals. Together they would make a great team for investing in real estate. Synergies like this can provide the basis for a very lucrative partnership.

Use your RRSP. If you are a first-time home buyer or have not been the owner of a principle residence over the past four years, you have the option of making the down payment of your home purchase using your Registered Retirement Savings Plan (RRSP) for additional cash. You are allowed to take $20,000 per person or $40,000 per couple out of your RRSP with no tax penalty as long as you are willing to repay prescribed amounts according to the schedule stipulated by the government. The amount withdrawn is treated as a loan and must be repaid within fifteen years starting in the third year after withdrawal. These funds can be used either to build or to buy a house.

Add Up the Hidden Costs

The asking price or negotiated purchase price for your home or project will not include all your expenses. There are hidden costs. Closing costs apply, such as legal fees, costs for conducting title searches, registration of title and registration of mortgages and credit lines, and other fees. In case your intention is to purchase a brand-new house, townhouse, or condo via assignment of the contract of purchase and sale, there could be an assignment fee as high as a thousand dollars or even more! Then there is the property transfer tax, which varies from province to province. For example, in British Columbia, this tax amounts to 1 per cent of the first $200,000 of the purchase price and 2 per cent of the remainder of the price. In Ontario this is called the land transfer tax. The land transfer tax in Ontario is calculated as the total of:

- .5 per cent of the total property value up to $55,000

- Plus 1.0 per cent of the amount from $55,001–$250,000
- Plus 1.5 per cent of the amount from $250,001–$400,000
- Plus 2.0 per cent of the amount in excess of $400,000.

However, first-time home buyers who plan to occupy the property as a princi-ple residence and who have never had an interest in a principal residence may forego the transfer tax within certain limitations.

When you buy new or substantially renovated real estate from a builder, or you construct or substantially renovate your own home, you will have to pay a goods and services tax (GST) of 6 per cent. A resale home is usually GST exempt, whereas if you buy a building lot as a holding property in a new subdivision, GST applies. However, you may qualify for a 36 per cent rebate of the 6 per cent GST if you plan to live in the house yourself or, as an investor, are willing to lease your property for a long-term lease of a minimum of one year. For new homes priced between $350,000 and $450,000 before GST, the GST rebate is reduced propor-tionally. New homes priced $450,000 before GST or higher would not receive a rebate. Special GST rebate application forms can be downloaded from the Canada Revenue Agency (CRA) Web site. Within approximately six weeks of dropping off your GST rebate application with the CRA, you can expect your GST rebate refund in the mail.

Hidden costs, though invisible at first, considerably add to the total of your purchasing costs, and you should have a rough estimate before signing binding contracts. To illustrate the importance of keeping your budget realistic when buy-ing real estate, and to show how considerable closing costs on a purchase transac-tion can become, read Paul's story:

Paul's Story

Paul bought a brand-new investment condo for $230,000. Three months later, the total cost of the purchase had escalated by $7,540. The lawyer's statement of adjustments showed the additional costs. First, a transfer purchase tax, calcu-lated on the purchase price less the GST, amounted to $1,950. Furthermore, an assignment fee of $1,000 was calculated as Paul had bought the new condo through an assignment of the contract of purchase and sale, meaning the devel-oper had originally sold the unit to another buyer who, in return, had resold the contract to Paul before the completion date of the building. The statement of adjustments naturally also included $550 in legal fees regarding the purchase, and $250 in legal fees regarding the credit line.

When Paul had his first walk-through with the developer, he noticed, to his surprise, that the living room floor was not level. It slanted down in the corner as well as in the middle of the room. This would need to be fixed by pulling back the carpet and pouring more concrete in two areas. Paul would be unable to have a tenant move into the unit until the flooring job was done. Instantly, the first month's rent revenue was lost. As 70 per cent of the purchase was financed with a credit line, Paul would now need to pay the credit line interest with no corresponding income—roughly $820 per month.

After the floor had been fixed by the developer, Paul had another month of vacancy, as it was December—a very difficult time to find a tenant.

To summarize, for two months Paul had all the expenses such as strata fees ($150 per month), advertising costs ($200 in total), credit line interest, and even property management fees ($75 per month; Paul used a property management firm to rent out his condo for him), and no corresponding income.

Finally, the developer had provided no window coverings for any of the units. This turned out to be another problem, because the tenants asked for window coverings as a condition for signing a one-year lease. As the condo was large and bright with huge windows, Paul spent another $1,500 on custom-designed window coverings. He decided he might as well install nice-looking pleated shades which would go well with all the other upgrades the unit already had, such as the tile entry and tile kitchen and the granite countertop. He figured that, at the time of resale, he would recoup this expenditure by being able to set a higher asking price.

So, it was two months later than expected that the first tenant finally moved into Paul's condo. Paul's expenses had escalated to a total of $237,540 for the unit, $7,540 more than the original purchase price! The monetary outlay for Paul during those first two months was even greater ($242,490) as he initially had to pay the GST rebate portion of $4,950 to the seller. Only after having signed a one-year lease with a tenant in the third month of ownership of the unit could he apply to the Canada Revenue Agency for a refund of the rebate.

Learn from this story: When you make the final decision on a purchase, budget for at least 105 per cent of the purchase price as your possible monetary outlay. In other words, calculate 5 per cent of the final sales price and add this figure on to your sales price to arrive at the amount of money you will possibly need to have at your disposition to financially carry through with your purchase.

Also, when (prior to your purchase of real estate) you try to calculate the future potential return or cash flow of the investment, add on a few percentage points to the purchase price (3 per cent or more) to take into consideration closing and other unexpected costs. This will prevent you from major miscalculations.

Paul's story also illustrates that you might encounter additional unexpected costs when purchasing units that are still under construction.

Conclusion

Finally, when you decide to take the plunge and invest in real estate, because of the financial magnitude of the investments, it is so important to buy only what you can truly afford. Don't overstretch yourself to the limit financially! Remember, sound real estate investing is generally long term and you need to have the funds available to see your investments through for the long run.

Stressful situations and financial uncertainty are unpleasant. With today's price situation, any investment in real estate needs careful financial preparation. It always pays off to be knowledgeable and well informed. The better you prepare yourself, the more likely you will reach your goals.

Key Points

❖ Diversify your investments.
❖ Consider owning a home and investing in real estate.
❖ Budget properly for your real estate investments.
❖ Beware of becoming financially overextended.

Chapter 3:

Investment Strategies

Perhaps your only goal is to own a home to avoid paying rent, while at the same time building equity. These would be your only concerns, and home ownership for you would be a place to call home and a place that, over time, would increase in value.

Different people have different objectives and employ different strategies to reach their goals. For example, you may buy a property and hold on to it for the long term with the expectation that the property will make money. There are investors who believe one should never sell, as, in the long run, real estate prices tend to appreciate. Other people like to try to time the market. They try to buy low and sell high. And then some people like to take a chance that, in a short period of time, their property will sell at an even higher price than what they originally paid, taking into consideration the purchase price and all the closing costs of the purchase and sale transactions. These three strategies are known as buying and holding, buying and selling, and flipping.

Buying and Holding

Buying and holding is what most people do. This means that you make a decision to keep your property for the foreseeable future with no intention to sell. Inflation will work in your favour and your property value will rise year after year if you plot it on a long-term graph that excludes the short-term action of market cycles. Over the long term, this theory works perfectly, as statistics prove over and over again. Once you have accumulated a fair amount of equity, you can refinance your property and buy more. The concept of buying and holding is well illustrated in Katherine's story.

Katherine's Story

Katherine lives in the house her grandparents built when they were in their best years. Katherine's family held on to the property for all those years. From what Katherine's grandparents and parents have told her, she knows how much lots and houses in her neighbourhood were worth in her grandparents' time and in her parents' time, and how much they are now worth. Over all the years, the trend in real estate prices was up and up and up.

Learn from this story: If you keep property in the family and do not sell to move on, over the years inflation will work wonders and the property value will definitely rise. Your local real estate board or agent should have no problem showing you the historical statistics for your area.

Buying and Selling

Another real estate investment strategy is to buy properties below market value and, at the right moment, with or without improvements, try to resell them at market price. This strategy can work well when you invest enough time to find good deals and generally are not in a hurry. For example, find a house that has been on the market several months and put in a lowball offer to determine if the seller is desperate to sell. Buy the house (if the price is right), and then ultimately resell at market price and pocket the profit. It is up to you if you want to do a bit of remodeling or renovating before you put the property back on the market.

Also, following the market closely pays off. Here, a strategy is taking advantage of the movements of the market. This could be financially very profitable—you buy when a market upturn is firmly established, which will be in a period where prices steadily move higher. You keep your property until you figure a market top could be close. Or, you try to put the property back on the market after riding the upswing for a while and you have already made sufficient money to invest in an even more promising project, or your financial situation allows you to split the risk within several properties. Such a steady uptrend in the market is most often established in times of good economic growth. The situation more or less correlates with high employment figures and low interest rates, which together lead to steady economic growth.

However, no upswing lasts forever. It is a good time to sell when you have a good profit or the market reaches a top. Local real estate boards have Web sites where they post market information such as in what direction real estate prices are going and whether it is currently a buyers' or a sellers' market. Many of the larger established real estate companies also feature Web sites that provide this type of data.

Flipping

The most risky strategy is flipping, which, to a large extent, not only depends on market conditions but also on your personality. It is not a wise strategy when the region is in a recession and market prices are falling, and it is definitely not a strategy for you if you are adverse to risk. Buying a property with the intention of flipping involves a lot more risk than buying a property with a long-term focus in mind.

Let's say you buy a property with the intention of flipping it soon thereafter. You take a chance and buy a property below market value. In this case, if you are not pressed for time, you should not have a problem reselling at market value. Then, if the sale price covers more than your original purchase price and the total of your expenses, your venture will be profitable. All you really have to do is wait for a buyer for whom your property might be, for any number of reasons, the ideal match to his or her expectations.

If you buy a fixer-upper, remodel it yourself, and perhaps put in new wiring, new plumbing, and so forth, you also could be successful. Yet, if you contract the remodeling out, renovations could take much more time and money than you anticipate. There are always the possibilities of labour shortages, extended delivery times, or running way over budget. Furthermore, flipping can be risky for the simple fact that the property may not flip fast enough before the market turns.

Flipping really came into vogue in the condo market. People bought into new developments at the pre-construction phase with only minimal down payments. By the time the developers had the building ready for occupancy, these investors sold their units with huge profits. This has successfully been done in project after project. With more and more equity, the opportunists move on and, indeed, they are coming closer and closer to the fulfillment of their dreams to really own a condo without debt, or to finally live in a condo in their favourite location. As long as there is a hot market and more and more of those very attractive projects—where sometimes the name says it all—are lined up over a short period of time, flipping seems so easy, it does look like a no-brainer. But as suddenly as this opportunity started, it will come to an end. In real estate terminology, a market bubble has been created and that bubble, sooner or later, will burst.

For argument's sake, let us say you are living in such exciting real estate market times that you just don't want to miss your chance to make a good profit. You are envious of some lucky friends who cashed in. Their success becomes infectious, and you want to buy too. When you buy a property with the intention of flipping it, make sure you buy a good value and, in your profit calculation, take into consideration the closing costs of both the purchase and the subsequent sale transactions. Moreover, don't forget to add in the interest you will pay for financing during the time the property is in your name. And calculate it for extended periods, just in case, when you cash in your profits, the completion of the deal takes a little longer than you had planned. Finally, you must keep an anxious eye on market and credit conditions all the time.

So, what happens really when profit-hungry investors storm into the showrooms of brand-new developments in different parts of your city? Impressed by plans and models, they buy directly from the builder before the construction of the project has even started. Here the idea is to resell with a substantial markup as soon as the project is built. The tremendous profits some of these investors have made in a very short time, with very little effort of their own, has been publicized well. And, as word spreads, people want to copy these success stories. One has only to look at the continuous streams of curious people who come when show centers of new and large developments open their doors. For the "Grand Opening Sales Weekend," developers now take appointments, with names and time of the day, in order to avoid the large queues. With possibly only 10 per cent down, the investor hopes that, in the time the project is being built, prices will continue to climb. Yet, who could know for sure what market conditions will be like at the completion date? If you pay down $30,000 on a $300,000 condo and you assume the price will rise 10 per cent yearly, the sales price will be $360,000 when the condo is in move-in condition in two years. This looks good on paper, but is this expectation realistic? First of all, your expenses have to be part of your calculations. Second, the full amount of that purchase price will be payable on the completion date without any guarantee of a successful resale. In addition, the investor will be pressed for a fast resale, because, from now on, interest expenses on credit lines or for mortgages add up, and there is competition because dozens of units were bought by investors with the same plan in mind, all at the same time.

Then there are those investors who don't want to wait for the completion date of the original contract of purchase and sale with the developer. They try to sell their contract of purchase even before the completion date of the project in order to avoid the full payment to the developer at that time. In this way, their only monetary outlay is the deposit they paid to the developer in the pre-construction stage of the building. As they "assign" their original contract of purchase to a third party before the completion date of this contract, they transfer the payment obligation they had with the developer to a third person. This third person purchases the original contract for more money, so the investor makes a profit. In other words, the unit is resold before the first owner of the unit is even registered at the land title's office.

It is quite astonishing to see the number of private resales or assignments of contracts on the MLS when it comes to large new developments just completed or close to being completed. This should make you cautious when deciding to take on the risk of purchasing a unit in the pre-construction phase of a brand-new development with the idea of subsequently flipping it.

Also, when buying any unit in the pre-construction phase, take a close look at the developer's history to make sure the project is likely to go through until completion and will not get stuck. Some developers have had significant problems with cost overruns, and financing difficulties due to the skyrocketing costs of labour and materials, resulting in delays and, occasionally, even a complete halt in the construction.

So you already bought a condo in the pre-construction phase from the developer. This time you thought you would like to live there yourself and make it your new home. What happens when, halfway down the road, you change your mind? This might happen if you get transferred to another job or you started the project with partners who got cold feet and left you with your obligations. George and Anna tell us their story:

George and Anna's Story

When George and Anna flew in from Toronto to go camping on the west coast, they found the area irresistible and decided to relocate. They bought a condo from a developer in August before the building of the project had even started. When the condo was three months away from completion, they were able to inspect it. They were very much surprised when the condo was, in their view, way too small for comfort in comparison to the beautiful, old character home they had called their own and had just sold. Then came a sunny weekend and the couple fell in love with a beautiful new townhouse in a different development out of town—just twenty kilometers more to drive, with green space in the back. They decided to put a down payment on the new townhouse without realizing how difficult it would be to quickly assign their contract of purchase of the condo. Under pressure to sell, they accepted an offer on the condo well below market value and assigned their contract of purchase of the condo to a third party.

Learn from this story: market value in this case is easily established—it is the price of other units with the same square footage and the same features in the same condo building that are on the market or have just sold. The building was still under construction when the couple changed their mind, so comparisons with units for sale or units recently sold should not have created a problem. There might be minor adjustments necessary because the comparable units may be on different floors or facing more or less desirable views. Of course, their real estate agent could have assisted them with these adjustments and, in general, would not have had any problem giving them information about market value. Real estate agents generally know their regions and should be able to explain any marked differences in the asking price and the expected fair value. Because George and Anna needed to get out of their original purchase of the condo fast in order to fulfill their new obligation with the townhouse, they sold at a bargain price although the real estate market at the time was sizzling hot!

Conclusion

Even if your intention is to flip a property, be aware that whenever you buy a property, you enter a legal obligation. For your own protection, sufficient and secured funds should be available at the completion date of your purchase. Investors have their very own personal and psychological profiles. Before you put money down on a project, make sure it has merit and fulfills your criteria. When you invest for the long term, you know your real estate investments will appreciate significantly with minimum risk. Equally, when you focus exclusively on good deals, you know you are ahead in the game. On the other hand, if you decide to speculate, you simply assume the next buyer will pay more as time progresses, yet the market could turn against you. If a real estate bubble bursts, the damage can be major.

> ### Key Points
>
> Decide on a personal investment strategy:
> * ❖ Invest for the long term.
> * ❖ Buy below or at market and look for deals.
> * ❖ Buy in an upward cycle.
> * ❖ When flipping, know the risks.

Chapter 4:

How to Spot Good Deals

To spot good deals, you must be patient and invest considerable time. Flag some properties that are of interest because of location, attractive design, or general affordability. But, definitively not everything advertised as a good deal will be good deal.

1. *Location, location, location.* Ask yourself questions like:
   - Is this a nice neighbourhood?
   - Is this a central location?
   - Is this a view property?
   - Is this an upcoming and growing area?
   - Is this an easy commute?

Nicole's Story

As was her usual routine on a Sunday morning, Nicole was flipping through the real estate section of the Saturday newspaper. She found an eye-catching ad for a new condominium construction project in an area of the city known to her for its urban renewal. The colour photo of the model was stunning. Moreover, the preconstruction prices were phenomenally low. When Nicole phoned the listing real estate agent, she learned that the building would have no expensive extras, no secured underground parking, no rooftop gardens, no storage lockers, and no granite countertops. The low prices of the units seemed comparable to the older condos in town.

Old, single-family homes were torn down at the location of this building site on the edge of the city, and nearby brand-new, big-box stores were already opening their doors and were ideal for shopping. There was a bright future for this part of town, yet most building plans authorized from a very progressive city hall were still on the drawing boards. A huge new hospital and a new branch of a large college would draw more people to relocate here and make this their home. Grocery stores, coffee shops, banks, and a movie theatre were all within walking distance of the planned condo building. Major retail stores had opened in this area over the last years such as Wal-Mart, The Brick, Costco, and Home Depot. Their employees would make great tenants. Furthermore, the commute to the downtown area of the city was only twenty minutes. As location is the number one determinant for people when choosing their residence, Nicole felt this would be a great investment.

Learn from this story: Here is an example of condominium units for sale in an upcoming and growing area of town. Location is the number one issue. Nicole's knowledge of general market prices for brand-new condominiums units also helped her spot this great investment.

- *Buy the cheap duckling among the swans.* It is better to buy the cheapest house in the best neighbourhood than to buy the nicest house in a run-down neighbourhood. Equally, it is better to buy the least expensive suite in an upscale condo project than the most expensive suite in a neglected building in need of tender loving care.

- *Why the big difference in prices for new developments?* Developers sell their huge new projects through a real estate agent of their choice. The developer's budget calculations may be oriented towards selling the complex fairly fast in order to recuperate financial outlays. To sell fast, prices can be moderate compared to the general market situation.

  Or, large projects could be cut into phases, so phase one, currently on the market, reflects current building prices, and phase two and three respectively will reflect future building prices.

  Or, the financing of a project is done in such a way that the developer is not pressed for time, but can ask the highest price the market can allow at any given time.

  The advertising budget of the chosen real estate agent will also reflect such considerations. So, generally speaking, there will be projects on the market priced moderately for fast sale and there will be those where the sellers take their chances to obtain higher prices. And all this has nothing to do with the quality of what is being offered.

- *Construction quality and design affect price.* When trying to find a good deal, you will see differences in construction quality and design. One certainly should not compare apples with oranges. The choices offered for materials in kitchens, bathrooms, and living rooms can show whether a builder adhered to high standards or not. Well-designed living spaces have a feeling of luxury, as decorators have been involved in planning the details of the spaces. For older housing, you need to add the upgrades into your own calculations to see if they really are good deals.

- *Know the market.* If you are looking for a house, familiarize yourself with a geographical area, certain types of houses, and the market prices. Calculate housing prices per square foot for specific areas, taking into consideration things like the square footage of the lot, the age of the house, and the size of the house. Allow a higher price for any extra upgrades and deduct dollar amounts for deficiencies or necessary repairs like a new roof. When you know the market inside and out, you'll know how to present an offer at or below market value, and consequently assure yourself of a good deal.

- *Be skeptical when too many "for sale" signs sprout up at approximately the same time.* It is wise to do some research and find the reason for this. Improvements by the community, like new water and sewer lines, are costly, and the property owners of the region will have to bear these costs. Suddenly, the fire-sale price on the last empty lot will not look so good any more. This kind of reasoning also applies when a new major highway is planned too close to a property.

- *Analyze facts about buildings that catch your interest.* Once you have set your sights on a certain condo project or subdivision where the resales are coming up more or less frequently, it is best to keep a list of the following information: the price range of all recent sales, statistics on square footage and floor plans, particulars like location in the building or in the subdivision, and days on the market. Now you should compare this information with the actual prices for which the units sold. Working closely with a real estate agent can help you analyze this information in a timely way. Attending any open houses will also help you to familiarize yourself, not only with layouts and views, but also with the condition of units and the sellers' motivations for selling. This will give you an idea on pricing for this particular development or building, and, when an undervalued unit comes on the market, you'll know right away and you can then act quickly.

Scott's Story

As Scott was driving to his friend's house he spotted a "for sale" sign in combination with an "open house" sign in front of a nice-looking condominium building. His curiosity won out. The open house condo was actually a show suite. A young assistant to the real estate agent handed him a price list. Construction would soon begin on a phase-two building, and they were selling this second phase, which would be identical to the one where the showroom was, so potential buyers could visit model condos.

The price list showed a variety of unsold units to choose from. One quick glance convinced Scott that opportunity was knocking—prices per square foot were close to what he had paid over a year ago for his first condo. This was totally unexpected, since real estate prices in general had risen significantly. Following the list down one by one he found that a two-bedroom corner unit on the second floor facing southwest was listed at $15,000 less than the identical corner unit on the southeast side. Furthermore, the condo was only $3,000 more expensive than the identical ground floor unit. Yet, the ground floor condo was right by the road and had no view, while this second-floor condo had a pristine view. The condo was a bargain. Scott had the impression that this condo was mistakenly priced low.

The layout of the unit was fabulous. It was a sunny condo, 780 square feet, two bedrooms of equal size, one big bathroom, a large living room with an electric fireplace, and a separate dining area. If he wanted, he could order the same colour combination as he saw in the show suite, and the same exciting design for the kitchen with that beautiful green granite countertop and the black appliances. Though the real estate agent's assistant had offered Scott a comfortable chair, Scott wandered around making himself familiar with this location. This was absolutely gorgeous. Best of all, from the living room he would have a fabulous golf course view with old-growth trees. While waiting to talk to the real estate agent, Scott saw deer roaming on the golf course in the late afternoon sunshine.

Nervously, Scott punched the numbers into his handheld calculator. It was true that the unit he had spotted was a great deal. How could he profit from it? This would be the chance of a lifetime. Then, he made an important realization: this condo still had to be built! He would not need to pay for it until its completion in spring of the following year.

Learn from this story: As Scott was familiar with market prices in the area from his condo purchase a year earlier, and, as he took his time to analyze the current price list, he immediately spotted the under-priced unit in this terrific location. He was lucky to stumble into such a great deal.

- *Understand price reductions.* Price reductions are not necessarily bargains. You should follow the price developments of properties that are of interest and notice any significant price reductions. It works in your favour to have an overview on asking prices per square footage, because in a hot market there are some very overpriced units for sale on which a reduced price would never qualify as a bargain. Here, some sellers' price expectations are not realistic and these prices have to come down in any case. You don't want to fall victim to a speculator. So, not every price reduction makes a good deal. Your buyer's real estate agent can inform you in this regard and can help you to find properties that are competitively priced.

- *Consider days on market when putting in an offer.* When, for prolonged periods, no acceptable offers come along for the seller, he or she may not only reduce the asking price significantly, but might also accept a low offer. To follow the pricing of particular properties of interest, the Multiple Listing Service (MLS) on the Internet (www.mls.ca) is very helpful. It is important that you are ready to secure a good deal when a good deal presents itself so that it is not lost to another buyer. There is very limited time to contemplate on a good deal in today's fast-paced markets. As soon as another buyer also spots the opportunity, you may be in for a bidding war.

- *Verify the promises advertising makes.* A last word of caution: do not believe all the advertising you come across without your own independent verifications. A good example is the case of a condo newly coming to market and advertised as "priced well below assessed value." A closer analysis proved this condo to be the most expensive per square foot of all the ten units for resale at the time in the building. It was the opposite of a good deal!

Fiona's Story

Fiona thought she had found a terrific deal. She was looking for a piece of land as a holding property. The prices for a building lot in Fiona's neighbourhood were too high for her budget. Therefore, she focused on land for sale farther outside the area, yet still participating in the real estate upswing. There were acreages for sale an hour away from the city in an area where $500,000 homes were the norm. Surfing on the MLS Web site for new listings, Fiona spotted a small acreage. The advertisement showed a nice photo with spectacular ocean view.

As it was the weekend, Fiona immediately got directions from the real estate agent and jumped in her car, expecting she had found a real gem. Driving the narrow, very winding road, Fiona passed through spectacular west coast scenery with high, old Douglas firs, arbutus trees, and ferns, and tiny, picturesque coves leading to a sheltered village.

However, when Fiona found the lot, she immediately realized that to show such a fantastic water view, the photo on the Internet must have been taken from the lot high above the one that was for sale. The lot that was for sale offered a rather poor view of the water—just a peek between a rooftop and some trees. Also, the distance to the ocean seemed significantly larger than she had expected as a result of studying that most attractive photo.

Learn from this story: When properties are advertised as beautiful, nicely land-scaped, having a fantastic view, or possessing other indications of a serene nature, it is best to see with your own eyes that these values truly exist. Sellers know that such superlative descriptions catch our attention, and, in a fast and competitive market, might trigger action. Imagine buying such a property "subject to viewing" and then flying in to discover the discrepancies.

Key Points

❖ Choose a good location.
❖ Buy good quality and attractive design.
❖ Know the market and buy below or at market value.
❖ Remember that not all price reductions signify good value.
❖ Consider days on market when making an offer.
❖ Don't believe all advertising. Verify.

Chapter 5:

Buying a Home, Buying an Investment

There are three conditions to keep in mind when purchasing real estate; never neglect one in favour of the others. Ask yourself: Do I like it? Can I afford it? Is it a good investment? There is a variety of reasons why you may wish to enter the real estate market at this particular point in time, but these considerations *always* apply.

Buying a Home for Yourself

Answer these three questions: Do I like it? Can I afford it? Is it a good investment? When buying a home for yourself, it is most important for your wellbeing and peace of mind that you like the new place and the chosen neighbourhood, and you feel happy and safe. "Location, location, location," is the first law in real estate and everybody knows it. Then, affordability becomes an issue. The following table demonstrates the variations in affordability in selected cities across Canada:

Table 4.1 Average Home Prices across Canada

City	June '06	June '07
Victoria	$538,913	$573,415
Vancouver	$508,435	$564,702
Calgary	$367,033	$427,205
Regina	$283,655	$315,332
Toronto	$358,035	$381,983
Ottawa	$260,458	$279,361
Montreal	$223,133	$235,087
Fredericton	$136,371	$153,063
Saint John	$127,586	$144,769
Yellowknife	$243,745	$314,022

SOURCE: Canadian Real Estate Association (*The Globe and Mail* August 4, 2007)[xi]

Before you sign a purchase contract, think about future resale possibility. In other words, even if you buy a home with the intention of keeping it for the long term, the property should also qualify as a good investment.

So you like the new place, you can afford it, and it is a good investment. Once you have these three conditions affirmed, you will have a better chance of avoiding "buyer's remorse syndrome," which so often happens to purchasers of real estate shortly after they have signed the contract of purchase.

Most times you must make compromises when choosing a property, as most homes include features you really like and features you care less for. It is very difficult to find the "perfect" home, which has all the features you wish for and none of the features that are less desirable. For example, you may find a lovely, end unit, one-year-old townhouse that features your dream designer kitchen with an island in the middle, large windows, and custom-made countertops; a living room with real hardwood floors; a family room with French doors; two four-piece bathrooms with skylights and slate tiling; and two very large bedrooms with windows facing a park. However, this townhouse end unit may be located right beside a noisy street, and its location would require a commute of half an hour over a very busy highway to the city. Moreover, the unit has a north-facing, less desirable patio and comes with a steep asking price. Or, you may find a lovely south-facing condo with spectacular views and a 150-square-foot balcony, but which has no natural light in the kitchen or bathrooms, making these rooms a bit dark. In essence, we must make compromises and decide what the most important features for us are, and which less-desirable features we are willing to accept.

Before buying that new home for your family or yourself, I suggest you create a list of the needs of everyone in your family. Once you have specified the needs, you should create a list with all the things that would make you happy if you *could* have them. As a result of your efforts, you will have two lists: a needs list and a wants list.

Figure 4.1 Home Buyer's Needs and Wants Lists

Needs	Wants
Maximum $450,000	New house
Three bedrooms	2500 square feet
Two bathrooms	Backyard for children and animals
Single level	Near playground
Outdoor environment	Close to parks and trails
A ready-to-move-into place	View
A neighbourhood where I feel at ease	Quiet street

Needs	Wants
Close to work	Wood floors
Close to school	Sunken living room
Close to grocery store	Wood-burning stove
Close to hospital	Hot tub
Minimal yard work	Granite countertops
Two parking spaces	Parking for RV

By identifying and writing down your needs and wishes, you can also give your real estate agent the perfect description of what to look for. You will certainly avoid being caught by a moment of irrationality, and being lured into signing a contract you later will regret. When you and your family have agreed on your home buyer's wish list and you are consequently buying a house you fall in love with, you will be happy because your choice was made from a sound, rational base of information.

Buying a Condo or Townhouse

Most of the above information also goes for buying a condo or a townhouse. But, there is a different catalogue of items to check off as well:

- Do you like the layout?
- Are you looking for a family-oriented building, an adult-oriented building, or a senior-oriented building?
- Do you need a pet-friendly building?
- Are you looking for a bright corner suite with lots of windows?
- Would you like a kitchen with a window and an eating nook?
- Would you like a two-bedroom unit to have the two bedrooms side by side or separately located on either end of the living room and dining room?
- Would you like a balcony off the living room, off the kitchen, or off the bedroom?
- Do you need an additional den to use as an office?
- Would you like one bathroom with a shower and another one with a tub?
- Would you like to face north, south, east, or west according to your preference for sun or shade?
- Would you feel comfortable on a higher floor or do you prefer a lower floor?
- Would you like to buy into a complex with recreational amenities such as a swimming pool, a fitness area, a rooftop lounge, or a workshop?

- Do you prefer a wood structure building which breathes more air or a concrete building which may be more fire safe? Or, is modern glass and steel construction your dream?
- Do you like high-rises or do you have a preference for low-rises?
- Would you like the property to be rentable with no rental restrictions in case you ever decide to move and do not wish to sell, or would you be more comfortable living in an all-owner-occupied building?
- Would you prefer an end unit with lots of natural light but with a higher heating bill in the winter?
- Would you feel safer with secured underground parking?

You have created an extensive list of your wants and needs in regards to your future home. Now is the time to also write up a list of features you absolutely do *not* want in your new home—issues you feel very strongly about. When you make your purchase decision, you may quickly review this list to make sure the property of your choice is really the right one for you. For example, if you prefer not to live in a rental-, age-, or pet-restricted strata building, when searching for a condo or townhouse, this should be the first question to clarify. Or, if you are sensitive to noise, you'll need to avoid any location near the highway or a major road, unless you have double-paned windows. Also avoid the unit next to the elevator or garage door. If you suffer from depression, you would probably benefit from a bright unit with lots of natural light and sunlight, and therefore you should shy away from north-facing units and units with few and small windows. On the contrary, if you are sensitive to the summer heat, a south-facing unit would be out of the question.

To guide you on your house-hunting journey, you need to have a clear picture in your mind about the features you wish to avoid or you simply cannot accept.

You should understand that a single-residence building may offer you a lot more freedom and privacy than any multi-family construction, as you don't have strata bylaws and strata rules and regulations to respect.

Once you think you have found your ideal home and you are ready to sign a contract, there is one last tip: picture the new place with your own style of furniture and disregard the accessories and furniture of the seller. There are special stage artists who know how to make a place look deceivingly attractive!

Having a House Built

If you want to build your own house, you obviously need a building lot. Generally, people look for empty lots. Sometimes nice and suitable places are already occupied by old structures, yet the value of the land merits your attention. In this case, the old structure may need to be torn down to make room for your house. If you have a certain type of house in mind, or you and your spouse agree on a certain architectural design from a construction company, you will have to make sure that the terrain is suitable for the characteristics of your building plan. If you are lucky enough to build with an architect, you could involve your architect in the search for the building lot.

Once you have found several lots you are interested in, it is time to start the building process. Here are the steps:

1. *Commit to a building plan.* Before you buy a building lot, you have to do a little research and commit yourself roughly to a building design and floor plan.

2. *Make sure the terrain is suitable.* Assess the plot for the feasibility of your chosen plans. Make sure the house fits onto the lot within the parameters legally allowed in that development or vicinity. Some developers subdivide their land into the smallest lots possible, aiming to maximize their profit by having a larger number of lots to sell.

3. *Assess additional costs of the building lot.* Building lots are not all equal. There are lots you can start building on without much extra cost, and there are lots that are expensive to build on. A level lot on good soil with no rocks or trees makes building easy. Having all services already installed to your site—water, sewer, power, phone, and cable—guarantees few additional expenses for utilities and services. The lots that promise the most additional costs are the ones where you have to cut down large trees, blast rocks to fit the house or driveway, or drill a well and put in a sewage system. Paving long driveways adds to the cost, and steep slopes add to the difficulties of putting everything in place. In the end, it might cost you thousands of dollars extra to get your dream site ready for building.

4. *Check zoning restrictions.* Familiarize yourself with the zoning of the land so you don't run into conflicts with your building plans. Are secondary suites allowed? Are detached garages and workshops allowed? Are fences allowed to keep your dog in the yard? There are lots of questions. In an area of small houses, your large design might be considered a monster house. Your building lot has to fit your plans and your plans have to

fit in the neighbourhood. There might be regulations on how small you can build and regulations on how large you can build. All lots have mandatory requirements and bylaws that you should be familiar with.

5. *Choose a builder.* There are good builders and there are builders who cut corners and don't adhere to excellence. Word of mouth tells you who is who. So make an extra careful attempt to talk to people who recently built their houses and have experienced one or the other variety. If you are new in the area, an easy way to find a good builder is through the Canadian Homebuilder's Association. You can choose a builder from their list of recommendations. Ask potential builders for references and check them out. Look at the places that attract your attention—not only from the outside, but also from the inside. The builder of your choice might be interested in your business and arrange for a tour himself if you let him know your concerns. If he is too busy to do this in person, he'll most likely send an agent to give you all the information you need and to win your confidence.

6. *Try to adhere to your budget.* Building your own home is an exciting and rewarding experience. Yet, when your dream home is taking shape, you have to be rather careful. Don't get overenthusiastic with a wish list for extras that have not been included in the initial plans. More often than not, budgeting means compromises between must-have and not-so-important choices. Additional costs must be balanced by cutbacks, or delaying aspects of the development to adhere to original financial guidelines. Of course, you could opt for lovely French doors and balance this expense with a lesser-grade carpet or a more affordable trim around the fireplace. Financing can also be stretched in regards to how you pay for the new house. The best deal is to pay when the roof is on and the keys are in your hands.

Buying for Investment Purposes

You may be interested in buying a second property as a long-term investment. From this rental property you would expect positive cash flow. You also may be interested in buying another piece of real estate for the short term because a favourable market situation has presented itself and you see an opportunity to flip that property for short-term profit.

Making money is clearly your top priority in considering an investment property. Your second priority may be to safeguard your capital. In either case, you need to find good value.

There are two paths to investing in real estate. The first path is to purchase an investment property for its potential appreciation. If you find a good deal, and hopefully you are not buying at a market top, over time you can expect your investment to rise significantly in value. The second path is to invest in a project that provides good income—positive cash flow is the key here. This means the rental income of the property covers most of the expenses associated with holding the property, such as property taxes, strata fees, mortgage or credit line interest payments, insurance, and repairs and maintenance. In addition, the income provides you with some monthly profit. (In Chapter 11 we'll be talking about renting out your property.)

Furthermore, there are various options of income and appreciation combinations within these parameters. For example, your new investment property may have a zero cash flow, meaning that the income just barely covers the expenses, but you are counting on a good appreciation due to the property's fabulous location or other attractive features that make it unique.

When you buy real estate as an investment, your life situation, the money you have, the time you have, and the knowledge you have about investing in real estate will make a difference in the choice that is right for you. If you are a busy professional, you might visit your financial advisor and buy Real Estate Investment Trusts (REITS). A more hands-on approach would be to find a newer condominium in a highly desirable location and have it leased through a property management agency. A good initial deal on the condo would help to set you up for a higher profit once you sell, but the special location would also lead to higher-than-average appreciation and lower-than-average vacancy. If you have some experience with building maintenance, you might want to buy a previously-owned condominium or house and put it back into good condition before reselling it for profit or keeping it as rental, which you then manage. It is best to have a business plan for your rental property, so your expenses are on target. If your choice investment is a fixer-upper, you have to be careful—new roofs, heating, and plumbing are expensive and, on the other hand, rent increases are legally capped at a maximum percentage per year. If you invest in a strata lot, strata fees could increase at a rate that soon overtakes your allowable rent increases.

Cash Flow

The argument that it is necessary to have, at all times, a positive cash flow from all rental properties is debatable. Positive cash flow is of the utmost importance for a *long-term* investment in a rental property, especially in a slow market or in a down cycle of the market. If the market is in an up cycle, with prices moving ahead at a vigorous rate, and you hold on to your rental property for a limited time, your outlook is different. If you conduct a feasibility study, your profit calculations will then have two components: first, rental income, and, second, the higher ultimate sales price.

To determine how profitable your investment will be, you have to know how much rent you can charge in relation to your purchase price. Then, on top of listing all your ongoing expenses, you also need a critical amount of money in a rainy-day account for non-budgeted expenses.

A rental property with a negative cash flow—where the rental income does not cover all the expenses such as mortgage or credit line interest, insurance, property taxes, strata fees, or repair and maintenance costs—could still make an excellent short-term investment, providing you can come up with the monthly negative cash flow through other sources of income. In the scenario of a rental property that provides a negative cash flow, you are betting on a quick and significant appreciation over a short period of time due to factors, for example, such as in-demand location or rezoning. Or, there is a chance you found a great deal at the time of purchase, like a property with an asking price well below market value. If you invest in high-end properties, top-floor condominiums, or expensive new housing, renting these units out is rarely the main objective. These units easily fall into the negative–cash flow category when rented. Here the ratio of the purchase price in relation to the potential rental income is very high and, therefore, taking into consideration the mortgage or credit line interest and property taxes, the result is a negative cash flow. These properties are expensive to purchase and there is a ceiling on the rent one can ask, considering the rental prices in the area for this type of property. However, they may make very good short-term investments despite the negative cash flow. Here a correct estimation of the direction of the overall real estate market becomes important.

Location

For investors in real estate there is a golden rule. We know it already: it is "location, location, location." Buying the cheapest house in a good location—in a good neighbourhood—is smarter than buying the most expensive property in an unattractive or rundown neighbourhood. Your investment will grow much faster in the good location and features such as ocean view, water view, mountain view, or valley view are in such great demand that you are virtually assured a higher-than-average appreciation and, thus, a higher return on your investment when you sell. Under the "location" category is the choice of city in which you buy. Real estate values in some cities or towns appreciate faster than in others. Cities are known for their different attractions and employment opportunities—some cities attract students with their universities and colleges while others attract government employees with their government headquarters. In cities that are more industry based, pollution may become an issue for residents. And then there are those beautiful towns that depend on the tourism industry for their existence. The cities that are in the news, alive and well, may be the cities that are growing, which means there will be continued demand for housing. Sports events such as the Olympic Games attract investments—nobody thinks that in a place like Whistler, where the 2010 Winter Olympic Games will be held, prices will go down.

Strategies for Investing in Condos

One look into the real estate section of a regional newspaper will convince even the most diehard skeptics that condominiums are hot items these days. One can partially blame this on the baby boomers, but it is possible to suggest that single-family homes have become so expensive that condominiums present a viable alternative. In my own estimate, the good economic times that we have enjoyed for several years make people hopeful that this process will continue. Consequently, they buy the wonderful new condominiums sprouting up like mushrooms in city centers in the process of marvelous urban renewal. Parents buy condos for their children when they start going to college, while well-employed young adults buy condos as investments and for their parents as a place to live during retirement. Stretched for time, young couples are among the top buyers of these centrally located, small, and efficient units.

Whatever the motive, these condo buyers have a nearly unlimited choice in location, style, and high-quality standards. The investor can follow different strategies to maximize profit. One such strategy is to purchase the cheapest unit in a building. When the investor wants to cash in, there will always be someone who wants to buy the most affordable unit. You may look for the cheapest unit on the main floor next to the elevator, or a one-bedroom interior suite, or a suite on top of the underground garage. To buy the best unit available would be another strategy, if you have no budget restraints. Usually the best units to live in are top-floor, corner suites—possibly with vaulted ceilings, skylights, or a rooftop balcony. Also good are units with large balconies and splendid views. In comparison to the less-expensive units, they generally have higher square footage and a greater number of larger rooms. With today's upgrades, these top-of-the-line condos can be exceptionally beautiful. At the time of resale, there will always be buyers trying to simply buy the best to reward themselves and to gain that special status.

A good investment idea is also a one-bedroom condo with a den. Dens are very versatile. They can be used as an office, a child's room, a playroom, a fitness room, a library, or a music center. If the funds are available, the price difference between the condo with the den and the one without becomes less significant. Newly divorced people with one child just love to rent these units, and it is often the first type of condo they can afford once they are in buying mode. There is a high demand for those units, which means higher-than-average profit margins for resellers.

Of course, there is no secret that different buyers are attracted to different features. For example, single female clients often find first-floor condos less desirable for security reasons, so their choice is a condominium on a higher floor. However, pet owners and gardeners love ground floor units with patios—the larger the better. Seniors in downsizing mode might also love to walk out onto their patio like they did previously from their old family homes. They may feel safer on the ground floor as they can no longer run down the stairs in case of a fire.

There is a general note of caution, though: when you buy a condo to rent it out for income purposes, you have to make sure that the strata bylaws allow this. Before signing a purchase and sales contract, you need to read the disclosure statement of the building to verify that there are no rental restrictions or rental quotas in place. You don't want to be placed on a waiting list until the condo can be leased. Of course, if you buy from the developer with no rental restrictions and you lease the unit out from the beginning, rental rights are grandfathered in regardless of later imposed restrictions by the strata council. However, as rules and regulations in the strata legislation continuously change, make sure that the grandfathered-in clause still applies to your project if you want to make use of it.

Condominium buildings can be managed either by a property management firm or by the owners on the strata council. For you as an investor, a condominium building that is self-managed might be a warning sign or a deterrent to buy. Self-managed condos are managed by their owners in order to save on professional management fees charged by property management firms for services such as strata management and accounting. So, if the strata council selects one or several of their own members to provide these services, you have to trust that these persons are knowledgeable and honest when managing the strata finances.

Problems that have been discussed in the news range from the owners' council saving money by taking shortcuts on insurance premiums to not putting enough money aside into a contingency fund. These practices create huge potential liabilities should a fire, flood, or earthquake strike the building. Or the owners on council may hire friends or family for significant repair and maintenance work required in the building, thereby foregoing the expertise of professional contractors in order to save money. You also would not feel good about strata council members getting away with not paying their share of the strata fees in exchange for their services to the council. Or, it would be a nasty surprise to find out that the strata's funds had been borrowed by family members and friends of other strata members and are not available to cover necessary repairs or costs the strata is incurring. The list of possibilities of irregularities is endless. As strata members are owners of condo units, they may sell and disappear. All of these potential problems definitely don't agree with the criteria of sound investment. Of course, any of these problems could easily be fixed—all that needs to be done is for the strata to come to the decision to employ a property management company to oversee the management and finances of the strata.

Cost-efficient Thinking

Most people go to quite some length when there is a chance to save money without compromising the big picture of their plans. Here are some thoughts on efficiency.

- *Think smaller.* Today's demographic trends show that family size is shrinking. This trend is reflected in the demands made on the real estate market. The typical Canadian family home could be a three-bedroom, two-bathroom home. When you are in the market to buy a house, this three-bedroom unit will also have a better resale value down the road when you have outgrown your home. The three- to four-bedroom house is what people will buy the most and what will most likely go up in value faster than smaller or even larger homes. On the one hand, this house will not compete with the two-bedroom condo market and, on the other hand, this house is more cost efficient to maintain and repair than a larger house. And, if financed with a mortgage, one does not pay interest for a room that one does not use. Of course, if the large old house is the only right location for you, and it is within your budget, you might consider creating a rental suite in the basement, for example, or upgrading the property in other ways that improve its value or provide additional income.

- *Be one of the first buyers.* If you can afford to buy new—and here it does not matter whether we are talking about a condo, a house, or a townhouse—it always pays to be one of the first buyers. In the new subdivision you can opt for your choice location. In a condo building you will have the best unit selection and you will be guaranteed the best price. Prices tend to be lower at the start of major projects because the developer has to secure financing for the project. In general, the developer will sell a certain number of units before construction starts in order to qualify for financing himself. Once this certain percentage of units is sold, the developer then has the option to (and usually does) increase the prices for the remaining units within a framework that reflects market conditions.

- *Adopt a wait-and-see attitude.* In a booming housing market, where the market becomes flooded with new construction, it might be better to have a wait-and-see attitude as a safeguard just in case the project you are interested in gets stuck in red tape, bad financing, or labour shortages and huge cost overruns. Also, buying at a later time—maybe in phase two or three of the project—will allow you to inspect the construction site and actually see and walk through identical units in phase one. Actually seeing what your money is buying can be rather reassuring, even though you may have missed out on a better price by then.

- *If you are a senior, evaluate different aspects of cost efficiency.* While, for the younger buyer, the financial picture might be of paramount importance, older or retired buyers might profit from quite different considerations. For example, if there is a bus stop in front of the house or condo and a supermarket and a community center next door, do you really need to own a car? In condo buildings, there is usually just one parking spot allocated to each condo unit. If you do not own a car, you can lease the parking spot quite profitably.

  In the newly acquired retirement home, you want to keep maintenance, labour, and costs at low levels. The physical work incurred in cleaning out gutters, cleaning windows, and removing ice and snow in winter can become cumbersome for seniors who live in single-family homes. Not having to worry about doing these chores or having to pay someone else to do them makes condo living an attractive alternative. Gated communities, such as gated condominium or patio home complexes, may also offer the additional security seniors often look for, allowing them carefree living and home security when traveling south during the winter months.

The New Condo Boom

With new condo construction going up everywhere, some analysts wonder if condos are overbuilt. For many years there was very little condominium construction. Hence, until now, supply has been catching up to demand. However, as far as the future goes, there is already the possibility of a glut of new condos in the marketplace. Supply may outpace demand. What would this mean for the condo investor? Well, ultimately, if supply were to outpace demand, condo prices would stop rising. Condo flipping would no longer be a profitable enterprise, and condo investment would lose some of its attractions compared to other investments. If construction costs were to remain high, and developers' profits were squeezed, possibly fewer condos would be built in the far future.

Conclusion

Having big dreams might be your first step to entering the real estate market, but only getting yourself prepared thoroughly will help you reach your goal. Put your objectives in writing. Create checklists of what to do and what not to do. Staying within your budget and making your dream come true at the same time may be more challenging to do than you originally thought, but, with the right tools, you can do it!

Key Points

- Buying a home:
  - ❖ Location. Location. Location.
  - ❖ Feel happy and safe.
  - ❖ Fit your budget.
  - ❖ Make a good investment.

- The process of buying your home:
  - ❖ List your needs.
  - ❖ List your wants.
  - ❖ List your dislikes.
  - ❖ List your compromises.

- Having your own house built:
  - ❖ Choose a house plan.
  - ❖ Find a suitable building site.
  - ❖ Consider additional costs to get the lot ready.
  - ❖ Choose a builder.

- Buying for investment purposes:
  - ❖ Location. Location. Location.
  - ❖ Have a business plan.
  - ❖ Aim for good value and appreciation potential.
  - ❖ Plan for income and positive cash flow.
  - ❖ Accept zero cash flow or slightly negative cash flow properties as short term good value investments if you can cover expenses with other funds.
  - ❖ Read rules and regulations, minutes, and financial statements of strata properties.
  - ❖ Condos are in vogue. Are they overbuilt?

Chapter 6:

Vacant Land, Timeshares, and Leaseholds

If you are interested in buying a building lot, or if you are considering investing in a timeshare, or if a leasehold is a convenient way for you to find a home, this chapter is written for you. It will help you with your decisions; the major points are clearly outlined.

Buying Vacant Land

In our time, empty land that is suitable for buildings is becoming scarcer. Supply and demand of vacant lots around towns and cities tends to be out of balance. Because of this, available lots are selling for astronomical prices. It is no wonder, then, that buying vacant land and holding on to it has been good for the property owner and has historically proven to be an excellent investment strategy. Investing in vacant land might be a particularly good choice if you buy land adjacent to a sea- or lake-side resort or a mountain development. Anything that stands out from your average lot will fetch a higher sales price in the future.

In general, more and more people move to urban centers, so demand always exceeds supply and there is little risk, if any, that land prices will ever decline significantly. Take a good look at your tax assessment notices. You will find that the land portion, over time, typically appreciates more than the building portion of your property. If your property is within an urban parameter, there is a logical necessity for price increases. If you inherit a small, old house somewhere close to a city center, the value of the house and the value of the land can become disproportionate to one other and a developer may step in to take advantage of the situation.

As property owners know all too well, year after year they must pay property taxes. This is no different for vacant land. But here, in general, the investor has no income from the land. This disadvantage is a major drawback. Also, if the land is financed and you have to pay interest on it, investing in a vacant lot might not be such a good idea after all. You must think twice if a land deal involves borrowed funds.

You may decide to move to a new subdivision where the developer sells all-inclusive contracts. In this case, it is the developer who bought the raw land and put in all the services: roads, water, sewer, power, telephone, and cable. When you buy the lot, it is fully serviced and there is an agreement made on the type of house the developer will build for you. Unless your intention is to flip the lot, you agree to very specific terms. These terms usually include a timeframe within which you have to decide which of the developer's designs suits your own needs and still is affordable. Depending on the market situation and the size and the concept of the new subdivision, the developer may accept to build according to a plan of your choice, be generous with his deadlines, or allow you to buy a parcel subject to the building codes of that subdivision, but with no other specifications. But, be aware that such an empty building lot might be taken over by the neighbourhood children as their favourite playground. Also, strata members will complain if weeds start growing uncontrolled, causing an eyesore and even a fire hazard.

John's Story

Looking to find an affordable lot, John turned his attention to rural areas. He considered a lot in a subdivision of roughly seventy lots. A piece of agricultural land had been subdivided and the lots had beautiful pastoral views of adjacent farmland. John fell in love with the area and began to picture his dream home built there.

The lots, however, turned out to be so small that most of the regular homes featured in a book of building plans would never fit on them! The developer had divided the land into tiny lots in order to maximize profits. Only very small houses could be built. The lots were barely 4,000 square feet—not the size and shape for John's dream home.

Learn from this story: Before making a buying decision, analyze the project in great detail. Not all building lots are equal.

Rural Land

If you are a born individualist and like to do things on your own terms, you might look for a nice parcel of land in a rural area. The farther the distance to urban centers, highways, cable services, and other amenities, the more affordable land becomes. Most often, land-use restraints also diminish with distance from urban centers.

If time and money play no role, and you are in it for the long term—for example, your retirement is ten years down the road—then you would be rather foolish if you did not buy a beautiful piece of property now on the market for sale. Make sure, however, that you know all the obligations that come with the land.

You might find affordable land that qualifies as a holding property, but remember that developing the land into building lots later will still involve substantial costs for permits, roads, and a complete infrastructure. You might be inclined to have this done by an experienced developer, which means that you would sell the raw land again. In this instance, the market might work with you or against you in terms of how fast and profitable your sale will be. It is essential to have an overview of all costs involved when considering the purchase of land as an investment, and to know that in real estate a good deal may take a lot of time.

When buying larger tracts of land, there are a number of important things to be aware of:

- *Be aware of shrinking lot sizes.* When a community puts in water and sewer lines, land use will be increased. This means lot sizes will shrink because people no longer need wells and septic systems. All of a sudden, the increased density of buildings will change the character of an area.

- *Inquire about ongoing or future projects in the neighbourhood.* These could take your view away once building starts.

- *Know land use regulations.* How close can you build to the water if your parcel borders a lake, a pond, or a river? Are there potential areas set aside for trees, plants, or animals? Are topographical features like slopes, rocks, or a creek beneficial or are they a detriment to building? Even the soil quality might affect overall costs.

- *Look for hidden cost factors.* If you are too far away to connect to communal water and sewage systems, have the property examined in regard to installing these necessities. Depending on the soil structure, the ability to install these necessities may be an essential issue for approval as a building site by the authorities. And it may turn into a major cost factor. You may want to condition the purchase of acreage on positive well drilling results (the availability of enough good-quality drinking water) as well as positive perk testing results. If you have to blast roads in rocky terrain or fill in swampy terrain you will be facing major cost factors too.

- *Ensure that the description and photos of the land that attracts you in the first place are accurate.* Photos might be taken from a neighbour's lot. In large developments, the view is often photographed from a helicopter. When buying a treed acreage it can be rather difficult to establish from which points you will have good views. Rarely do all sites enjoy the same good views. If you consider construction on a steep area with northern exposure, hours of sunshine will be minimal.

- *Vacant land may not be for the inexperienced investor.* To buy vacant land in order to put in a development bears considerable risks. Time as a risk factor in a hot market is just the most obvious. The hotter the market, the greater the window of opportunity. But, will your development be ready before the market turns down? Disappointment and bankruptcy can lurk around the corner.

- *Some investors gamble on rezoning.* There are astute investors who buy cheaper residentially zoned land with the expectation that, one day, rezoning of the land will allow for pure condominium development, or, even better and more profitable, condominium development including some commercial space on the ground floor. Here again, time can play against you if you need to hold on to the raw residentially zoned land for many years with no corresponding income and hefty property tax payments until one day in the far future you may or may not be allowed to develop this land with a condominium complex and/or commercial space.

Timeshares

With the buoyant economy, timeshares are becoming more widespread than ever before. The timeshare vacation property market is in strong demand by the baby boomer generation. When baby boomers invest in a vacation property, they not only think of themselves, but consider their entire families—children and grandchildren. They buy into a recreational property so that, together with their large family, they can enjoy vacationing there. Investment potential often seems to be only a secondary consideration.

This section looks into your timeshare as a second home, as an investment, and as a convenient place to bring the whole family together on vacations. You will learn about the most attractive features and some insight into the drawbacks when it comes to associated expenses or reselling your timeshare.

You might fall in love with a timeshare because it guarantees you a certain luxury and lifestyle. The developers of these vacation properties usually lure the public interest with fantastic photos of their projects. Promotional advertising knows no limits when it comes to selling those dream vacations where you can make the most of your quality time. Although we are flooded with beautiful brochures, there are some features of the timeshare that everybody should know before starting the adventurous ride.

A timeshare may be the right investment for you if you buy it for your own personal use and enjoy vacationing at the same place and at the time during which the timeshare is allotted to you. This is the reason that a timeshare may be especially suited for retired people or people who know they can get the time off work when their timeshare is available to them. Of course, you also have the option of renting out your timeshare either through a rental pool or the on-site property manager during the times you are unable to come. However, when your timeshare forms part of a rental pool, in the event you wish to stay at your timeshare, you need to book your own place well ahead of time, following the hotel or property manager's regulations. It is relatively difficult to show up at the spur of the moment with the expectation that your own unit will be available for you.

With a recreational home such as a timeshare, you'll get to know the other owners of the complex who have the same rotation as you. In this way, your property will feel like a home away from home. The recreational amenities are usually exceptional and can include a restaurant, lounge, library, one or more pools, whirlpool, steam room and hot tub, or even an entire spa and tennis courts. The setting may be breathtaking, with ocean or lake views, on a golf course, or in the mountains. Or you may have a unit in a ski resort. The interior designer packages may come with granite countertops, stainless steel or black appliances, solid maple or oak furniture, oversized soaker tubs, king-size beds, and leather sofas and chairs. The designers pride themselves surrounding you with every imaginable luxury.

If you want to buy a brand-new timeshare, it may be cheaper to buy directly from the developer in the pre-construction phase rather than buying a private resale later, as most private resellers want to make some profit on their investment. During the pre-construction selling phase, showrooms are open for a registration process, which usually involves a moderate down payment and guarantees you the best choice. After your initial purchase cost, you have to pay monthly maintenance fees, which are stipulated by the company (perhaps a major hotel chain) that will run the timeshare.

Fractional ownership can go anywhere from one week per season to ownership of one eighth, one quarter, one half, or full ownership of the unit. Some timeshares give you the choice to purchase the winter season, the remainder of the year, pre-season, full season, or late-season.

If, for any reason, you cannot use your allotted time and know this ahead of time, you can assign your timeshare to be rented out by the property management. As much as 40 per cent or more of the rental income may be kept by the management company. For an investor, this may not be a very good deal. The high fees go towards maintenance costs including everything from room service to renting your place to hotel guests, to replacing broken dishes (for the latter a special fund is usually set up).

Should your timeshare be bought out by a hotel chain during your ownership, you'll face additional setup costs to accommodate all the changes necessary to be in line with the policies and regulations of the new hotel chain. On the bright side, you are able to generate revenue by renting your vacation home when you are not there. However, keep in mind that your unit may be fully rented in the summer months, around Christmas, and any other holidays, while remaining empty during the rest of the year.

Units in brand-new timeshare developments tend to be very expensive. In British Columbia, for example, in the spring of 2007, the original price for a typical timeshare ranged from $75,000 for a studio or one-bedroom unit to $300,000 for a two-suite lock-off. Multiply these figures by four and you'll get a price of $300,000 to $1,200,000 for full ownership of a luxury recreational condominium. These prices are high compared to the outright purchase of a condo outside of a recreational timeshare property. In other words, when buying recreational property you pay a steep premium for all the amenities available—for the luxury of the suites, and for the professional management of the property.

Selling your timeshare will be a very different matter and will not always be easy. When brand-new timeshares come on the market, they usually come with a very intense promotional package. Buyers are enticed by glossy brochures and state-of-the art promotional strategies. However, when you yourself wish to sell your second-hand timeshare, things are rather different. Your advertising possibilities are more limited. Also, you are selling to a very limited number of people interested in buying an existing timeshare, as most potential timeshare buyers are still lured into the brand-new glittering projects. If you have ever looked at all the timeshares for sale on the MLS, you will have seen a great number of them sitting there for months and months unsold. This said, an older timeshare may be considerably more difficult to resell than a unit in a relatively new and luxurious complex. Experience shows that people who can afford such luxury buy their units when they are new on the market.

If you are considering buying a timeshare as a revenue property, first make up your mind whether you really want to be in the business of recreational property—possibly even in the hotel business—or if you prefer the straight forward business of renting out a regular condo. If you decide to own a vacation property that generates income through a timeshare structure, understand that this business has its own set if rules. For example, your property taxes could be multifold when your property falls under the hotel category. Furnishings and equipment in your unit have to comply with hotel standards and regulations, especially if your timeshare is managed by one of the large hotel chains. Various factors can influence your income from your timeshare, such as the weather, tourism trends, or even such things as the currency exchange rate. So the income you receive from your timeshare is not easy to forecast ahead of time, and average income figures from prior time periods do not necessarily give an accurate picture of what you can expect in the future. Therefore, your rental income will fluctuate from month to month, from season to season, and from year to year, depending on the occupancy rate of your suite.

Leaseholds

Leaseholds—holding properties through leases—are a distinct class of real estate not everybody is familiar with. Leaseholders never own land, and buildings on the land cannot be passed on through inheritance to coming generations. Leaseholds do stand out as a special category of real estate. When you browse Web sites for properties for sale, you may find houses, townhouses, and condos listed at much lower prices than you would expect. If any one of these listings fits your objectives, pay attention to whether or not it is a leasehold. Ask your real estate agent to explain to you the difference between free-title holdings and leaseholds before you arrange any viewings or other specific inquiries. Leases usually run for a prolonged period of time—one hundred years, for example. At the end of the lease period, you own nothing. The original owner can take over the use of his land with everything on it, or he can negotiate a new lease. However, negotiations of renewal are often tough or may be unreasonable as the value of land increases tremendously over the lifespan of the lease. If a leasehold attracts your attention and would fit your budget, then you need to know how many more years remain in the lease before it expires. You might enjoy this remaining time;

yet, at the end there will be uncertainty and your lease may increase multifold if it is continued at all.

Leases "for life" are seen often in retirement communities which offer a great array of services to seniors.

Conclusion

First of all, when you buy vacant land, make sure the use you intend for the land matches with zoning and regional regulations.

If you are a very creative individual, you can start out with a building lot and then choose your own house design. A lot also could be a great investment for your future retirement. Buying a piece of land/acreage could be of special interest if you have surplus funds available, so you would be able to invest your own money. With no income from an investment in land, and the need of yearly property tax payments, you certainly don't want the additional obligation of interest payments, which would be the case if you were to buy the land using financing.

In case you plan to use the land as a holding property, make sure the developer or seller allows this and there is no time-limited building obligation tied to the purchase contract. If you get a chance to participate in developing land for construction, there are many pitfalls for the inexperienced, yet such properties can make you a fortune.

If you are thinking of buying into a timeshare property, picture yourself buying a regular and permanent vacation home—a home away from home. Have a long-term vision in mind, with income or investment considerations only as a secondary objective.

And, finally, if you are looking only for a place to live, a leasehold is more affordable than a free-title property. However, know that if you have beneficiaries, such as children, grandchildren, or a spouse, and you wish to leave them something, at the end of a lease term there is nothing to give away by inheritance. Equity has been replaced by affordability.

Key Points

- Building lots:
  Advantages:
  - ❖ Demand outpaces supply. Great appreciation in value.
  - ❖ Location influences resale value.
  Disadvantages:
  - ❖ No income.
  - ❖ Property tax payments.
  Varieties:
  - ❖ Lot size.
  - ❖ Raw land.
  - ❖ All serviced lot.
  - ❖ All inclusive contract: i.e., building contract.
  - ❖ Inherent characteristics of land.
  - ❖ Land use regulations.

- Timeshares:
  Attractions:
  - ❖ Amenities.
  - ❖ Luxury.
  - ❖ Second home.
  - ❖ Ready to enjoy.
  - ❖ Secondary objective: an investment.
  Financial considerations:
  - ❖ Very expensive per square foot.
  - ❖ Very high monthly maintenance fee.
  - ❖ Irregular and unpredictable income.
  - ❖ Hard to resell.

- Leaseholds.
  Advantages:
  - ❖ Cheap. May fit your budget.
  Disadvantages:
  - ❖ Lease expires. Then you own nothing.
  - ❖ Uncertainty when renegotiating lease.

PART TWO:

THE PROCESS OF BUYING PROPERTY

Chapter 7:

Mortgages and Credit Lines

While Part One of this book looked at the aspects that have to be considered and, in general, may be of interest when you are looking for property, Part Two deals with the process of buying property.

When buying your own house, townhouse, or condo, one of the first things you have to do is to establish how much money the bank will lend you for your project. This chapter will discuss a variety of mortgages and payment plans you can choose from. Lending experts look at your financing needs from different points of view. Knowing these differences may save you a fair amount of money and enable you to ask very precise questions when you meet with the mortgage specialist. This chapter will also tell you why it is beneficial to have a personal banker, and the great advantage of having pre-approved financing in place.

Have your last year's notice of assessment at hand in order to show that you don't owe any taxes. Any financial institution has an obligation to make sure that you are up to date on your income tax payments before they get into negotiations for a mortgage or credit line with you. You have to pay the Canadian Revenue Agency first if you are in arrears, or you will not be eligible for bank financing.

The Personal Banker

It is very helpful to have a personal banker. Banks not only want to do business with you, they also will establish your financial client profile which is rather advantageous for you and facilitates and speeds up the lending process. The better the business relationship with your banker, the better the purchasing process will be for you. The personal banker is the person who makes things happen for you. Furthermore, he or she bases decisions on in-depth knowledge of your financial background. If the professional relationship is well established, more often than not a phone call is all that is necessary for you to know if you can go ahead with a deal, or if your plans are too ambitious. Your personal banker can see, with one glance at your file, how well you do financially. In order to approve your financing needs, your personal banker will immediately be able to tell you what kind of documentation is needed. You will know how much financing you can get, and this will speed up the process. On top of this, you will most likely qualify for preferred client status which will assure you the best available rate.

Low-Down Payment Mortgages

You are afraid the real estate market will continue to go higher, and owning your own home will become unaffordable if you wait any longer. So you want to enter the market now and take your chances. You are convinced that this is not the right time to wait, and try to save more money for a larger down payment in the future. You think the market is moving so fast that affordability could dwindle. Assuming you can come up with the money for a 5 per cent down payment, you can now apply for a federally insured mortgage with the Canadian Mortgage and Housing Corporation (CMHC).

A low–down payment mortgage is one in which you ask the bank for an amount of money that exceeds 80 per cent of your home's purchase price (you offer less than 20 per cent as a down payment). This is also called a high-ratio mortgage. With this type of mortgage, the bank will ask you to buy mortgage insurance, which offers protection in case you should become unable to make payments. Over time, the insurance cost for this high-risk borrowing will add to your overall costs quite substantially. The lower the down payment, the more you need to pay on insurance. To avoid this situation, you need to put down a higher down payment.

So what are the risks involved in these low–down payment mortgages? Traditional mortgages are calculated over a twenty-five year period with specific conditions renewed after a specific term according to your personal agreement with the lender. Here, the first risk is that, over time, increasing interest rates will amount to such a burden that you may have a problem continuing to pay them. The case is that, when real estate prices go up and up and up, at one point, the central bank steps in and raises interest rates so inflation will not get out of hand. Step by step, mortgage rates that are not locked in for a prolonged period also follow this upward trend.

When you think you can no longer afford to pay your mortgage, everybody else will be in the same boat. At this level, there are very few buyers for real estate. Subsequently, property prices decline. Your second risk thus becomes evident when the market cycle had reached a top and enters a period called a market downturn. Once this trend is firmly established, the equity of your property will also decline. If the decline in the value of the property you bought is significant, the bank will become worried and will ask you for additional funding, so that lending ratios will match your original mortgage agreements again. At this point you may consider changing the terms of your mortgage, say from a thirty-year amortization to a forty-year amortization, or, through other changes, you might be able to achieve more breathing space (which will make your home more expensive over the long run). If you are forced to sell into a declining market because the equity of your investment has substantially declined, you could experience a considerable financial loss.

Market conditions can easily change and can seriously afflict your financial health. As you are now familiar with these risks, ask your financial institution to carefully explain each step in financing your property purchase before you sign any documents. An institutional mortgage specialist will be eager to get your business. As mortgage conditions and regulations change with a changing real estate market, your specialist will give you all the advice you need.

In past real estate cycles, a down payment of 20 per cent or more was the norm, so people had a little bit of a cushion for market swings. With today's high leverage, everything becomes faster and risks are higher. During the last severe real estate downturn—in the 1980s—homeowners across Canada who could not keep up with their obligations to their financial institutions simply handed over their house keys. Homeowners were shocked that such disaster could happen to them!

No-money-down Mortgages

When you take out a no-money-down mortgage, your bank gives you credit for the entire purchase price of your property. This means that you don't even need to pay the minimum 5 per cent down payment usually required for federally insured mortgages by the Canadian Mortgage and Housing Corporation. You can apply through the CMHC to purchase a house with no money down if it is your principle residence. Moreover, to be eligible, you need to prove to your bank that you have sufficient income and a secure job to cover the higher mortgage premiums. To qualify, your credit rating also needs to be excellent.

With no equity in your home, working with this type of mortgage leaves you very vulnerable to any real estate market downturn. This inevitably exposes you to the risk of your bank or financial lender asking you for more money down the road in the event of a market decline. The bank has to maintain a certain ratio of financing compared to the value of the property financed. Again, if the value of the property against which the mortgage or credit line is secured declines, you have to make up the difference by coming up with additional cash. If you cannot come up with the additional funds, you may be forced to sell your house at a less-than-an-ideal price.

Cash-back Mortgages

A cash-back mortgage is essentially a type of no-money-down mortgage. As the name indicates, when you sign this type of mortgage, the bank will put at your disposal a certain amount of cash that you may use at your discretion. For example, you may use the cash to pay your lawyer's fees, to cover your moving costs, to purchase your furniture, and so on. The amount of cash you receive is based on the size and the term of the mortgage you select. If you are interested in this type of mortgage, ask your lender what the applicable interest rate would be before making a decision to sign up.

Choosing a Mortgage: Fixed Rate versus Variable Rate

When you sign up for a mortgage, you need to decide whether a fixed-rate mortgage, a variable-rate mortgage, or a combination of both—a hybrid mortgage—best fits your needs. Many people find it difficult to make the decision between a fixed-rate and a variable-rate mortgage, and the majority of people still sign up for a fixed-rate mortgage. The results of a survey by the Royal Bank show: "Most Canadians are confused about variable-rate mortgages, with three-quarters thinking they will result in variable payments should interest rates change."[xii]

And, as stated on Canadian Broadcasting Corporation (CBC) *Report on Business News*, the most popular mortgage among Canadians is the five-year, fixed-rate mortgage. Furthermore, 73 per cent of all Canadians chose a fixed-rate mortgage over a variable one.[xiii]

With the variable-rate mortgage, as the name indicates, the interest rate may vary from month to month, but the advantage is that generally you pay a lower rate than you do with a fixed-rate mortgage. Does it mean that with a variable-rate mortgage you never know how much you pay each month until the bank sends you your statement? In most cases, absolutely not. Month by month, you will pay a fixed amount, but the amount of your payment that goes towards interest and the amount that goes towards principal changes when interest rates change. When interest rates rise, your payment pays off more interest than principal; when interest rates fall, your payment pays off more principal than interest. However, to be on the safe side, have your banker or mortgage broker explain the variable-rate mortgage that is offered to you, as some lenders still have variable-rate mortgages on which the payment varies when rates change.

When you start your mortgage payments, you will pay less interest without a doubt when you have chosen a variable-rate mortgage; but, in an environment where there is a trend for increasing interest rates, you probably are better off with a fixed-rate mortgage. The variable-rate mortgage may be cheaper initially, but could be riskier than a fixed-rate mortgage. To solve the dilemma and be in a position to make an informed decision about which type of mortgage would suit you best, try to follow the news to determine which way interest rates are heading. If there is talk of renewed inflation fears and/or a heated economy, you'll know that there is a possibility of rising interest rates in the near future, while, in general, during a recession, interest rates go down.

A good source of information about the most likely direction of interest rates is your report on business, either on television or in the newspaper. Your bank may also send you a quarterly newsletter that includes this kind of macro-economic information. Even with an established trend, nobody knows for sure when or how much interest rates will go up or down.

Economists and business people carefully watch the prime rate. The prime rate is set by the Bank of Canada (central bank) based on a broad range of economic factors. The central bank's mandate is to keep inflation low. In order to keep inflation at the low target rate, the central bank may raise interest rates. If you follow the news closely, you will hear economists talking whenever rate changes are expected, because this information as a cost factor is very important for the overall economy. If interest rates are in an upwards trend and there is a probability that they will continue to rise for some time, locking in a fixed-rate mortgage rate will save you money. If interest rates are stable or have a trend towards getting lower, going with a variable-rate mortgage would be the better alternative. You can switch any time from variable to fixed term conditions in an environment of rising interest rates.

Fixed-rate mortgages	Variable-rate mortgages
most popular	less popular
higher interest rate at start of the term	lower interest rate at start of the term
higher initial payments	lower initial payments
ideal if interest rates increase	ideal if interest rates stay the same or decrease
less overall risk	more overall risk

Hybrid Mortgages

Hybrid mortgages are another option. This mortgage features the combination of a fixed-rate and a variable-rate in certain proportions and is tailored to meet your specific needs. In fact, you yourself decide on the percentage split. The variable rate portion enables you to take advantage of current low rates, while the fixed portion protects you from future rate hikes. In this regard, financial products vary from one lender to the next. For example, 60 per cent of your mortgage could be fixed for a term of three years while 40 per cent of your mortgage could have a variable rate for three years.

Short-term versus Long-term Mortgages

The term of a mortgage agreement can range from six months to ten years or more. The general rule is: the shorter the term, the lower the rate, and the longer the term, the higher the rate. If you find yourself in a trend of rising interest rates, you might consider locking into today's rates for a longer term. With falling rates, a shorter term will be more beneficial for your pocketbook. Again, the columnists of the business section of your newspaper make it their job to inform you where interest rates are heading. Knowledge of interest trends is paramount for making decisions about your mortgage.

As an example, with an amortization period of thirty years and a term of five years, the terms of a mortgage would come up for renewal five times over that amortization period of thirty years. A fixed-rate mortgage for this term would carry a fixed interest rate for each five-year period. There are times when it is advantageous to have a variable rate. Variable rates are tied to the prime rate. The contract with a lender shows prime rate minus so many basis points. This means that the interest rate on the mortgage will reflect each incremental step the Bank of Canada moves the prime rate; thus, it will vary with the prime rate. Yet, the borrower's specifically negotiated deal with the lender—say one hundred basis points below prime—will stay unchanged.

Open versus Closed Mortgages

The advantage of an open mortgage is that you may make payments of any amount at any time without a penalty. This type of mortgage could be of interest to you if you decide to flip the property you are mortgaging or, in general, think of selling soon. It is also something to consider if you expect to receive a large amount of money from another source of income; for example, an inheritance or proceeds from the sale of another property. Such funds could be used to lower your mortgage without penalty.

You could get a variable-rate open mortgage at prime rate; however, with a variable-rate closed mortgage, rates tend to be below prime and therefore are more attractive. Remember, when you opt for that closed mortgage and then wish to make any lump-sum payments above pre-set limits, you will be charged with penalties.

Mortgage Payment Schedule

There are ways to pay down your mortgage faster and to save on interest payments. If, over time, you earn a higher income or, for whatever reason, have more funds available, you could look at your prepayment options, or you could change your payment schedule from monthly to semi-monthly, bi-weekly, or weekly. Paying mortgages off bi-weekly or weekly takes years off your payments in comparison to monthly payments. This is because you'll be paying less interest over the term of the mortgage. You could save a lot of money. The following table shows the savings you can achieve by choosing semi-monthly, bi-weekly, or weekly payments rather than monthly payments for a mortgage of $230,000 with an interest rate of 6 per cent amortized over forty years:

Table 7.1 Different Payment Schedules

	Amount	Amortization	Total Cost	Savings versus Monthly payments
Monthly	$1,254	40 years	$371,766	0
Semi-Monthly	$627	39.8 years	$368,748	$3,018
Bi-weekly	$579	39.4 years	$362,390	$9,376
Weekly	$289	39.3 years	$361,066	$10,700

Limits to prepayments are important. Different lenders offer different prepayment options. How much are you allowed to prepay per year without penalty? Is it 15 per cent per year? Or is it 20 per cent per year? Your prepayment terms are an important factor to consider in choosing a mortgage and a lender to work with, especially if you are expecting a lump sum of money to come your way in the near future. The greater your financial flexibility, the easier it is for you to adjust to changes in personal or economical conditions over the term of your mortgage.

Amortization Period

The amortization period of a mortgage can be as short as fifteen years or as long as forty years. Mortgages with thirty or forty year amortization periods essentially enable you to enter the market at an earlier stage when you may still earn less income, because your monthly premiums will be lower. With lower monthly payments, there is less chance that you will default on the monthly payments.

On the other hand, the shorter the amortization period, the quicker your home will be mortgage free. The greatest advantage is not only to be mortgage free faster, it is also that the total cost the mortgage will be less. Your property is less expensive with a shorter amortization period. For example, if you pay off your mortgage in fifteen years instead of twenty or even thirty years, you'll be making higher regular mortgage payments, but you will save yourself a lot of interest over time. The following table compares the mortgage payments for a fifteen-year, a twenty-year, and a thirty-year term mortgage at a 6 per cent interest rate on a property bought at a cost of $230,000 with a down-payment of 5 per cent ($11,500), and annual property tax payments of $1,500.

Table 7.2 Costs of Mortgages of Differing Durations

Property cost	$230,000		
Down payment 5 per cent	$11,500		
Loan term	15 years	20 years	30 years
Interest rate	6 per cent		
Annual property taxes	$1,500		
Monthly mortgage costs	$1,844	$1,565	$1,310
Monthly mortgage insurance	$102	$118	$142
Total monthly mortgage payments	$2,071	$1,809	$1,577
Number of months in loan term	180	240	360
Total paid over term	$372,780	$434,160	$567,720

As you can see, the longer the term, the lower the monthly premiums, but the higher the total cost of the mortgage over the entire term.

Mortgage Life Insurance, Creditor Insurance, and Critical Illness Insurance

You have the option to buy mortgage life insurance. This insurance will pay off the amount outstanding on your mortgage in the case of your death.

Another insurance option is creditor insurance for your mortgage. This covers mortgage payments any time you are unable to make mortgage payments due to illness, unemployment, or other circumstances.

Finally, you can opt to buy critical illness insurance to cover mortgage payments in the event that you become ill with cancer or suffer from a heart attack or stroke.

Home Credit Lines

A credit line is secured against your property and registered just like a mortgage at the land title office. The rate of your credit line is equal to the prime rate established by the Bank of Canada. You may qualify for a line of credit up to 75–90 per cent of the value of your home. Should you be unemployed at the time, you may still secure a credit line up to 65 per cent of your equity with no verification of income other than last year's tax return as proof that you are up to date with all of your income tax obligations.

A home line of credit is more flexible than the traditional mortgage, as all you need to do is make monthly interest payments. Once your monthly payment is taken care of, how much of the line of credit you pay off and when you do so is then entirely up to you. Whenever you have funds available, you can pay your credit line off in one big swipe. The nice thing about a credit line is your total flexibility. Of course, the more you pay off, the less interest you pay, and, at the same time, you increase your ownership and build equity. The advantage over the traditional mortgage is that you are not restricted to a payment schedule of monthly mortgage payments. To enjoy this total freedom, you may pay higher interest than with a mortgage, but you avoid the payment of penalties and the renegotiation of terms.

When you decide to sell the property and pay off the credit line, there will be a small fee for the closing of your credit line—for example, $75—but there are no penalties, unlike a closed mortgage on which you pay a hefty penalty unless you are able to transfer your mortgage to your next property. Transferring a mortgage to your next property is often difficult to do as the bank puts a sixty- to ninety-day time constraint on finding, purchasing, and applying the old mortgage to a new property. As you become a seasoned investor, you will know how difficult it is to find your dream home in sixty days! In reality, you would have had to purchase a new home subject to the sale of your old home—with all the related difficulties such a deal brings with it—in order to have the existing mortgage transferred onto your new property.

So, while a home credit line may tie in better with your personal financial situation than any of the amazing number and variety of mortgages, there is still another advantage. Once you have started paying down your credit, you can go back to the full established limit. This means that, if you were again in a position of needing more credit, you could take out your full limit without anybody from the bank asking questions. More importantly, the interest of a home equity line of credit is much lower than on regular personal credit. This is because the bank has secured the credit with your property. Therefore it may be financially advantageous for you to consolidate your entire household debt into this credit line. Whatever you decide, your main goal should always be to carry less debt—or even become debt free—and to build equity to secure your future and that of your family.

To illustrate a situation where the use of a credit line rather than a traditional mortgage became ideal, let us look at the story of Pauline and Ernest:

Pauline and Ernest's Story

Pauline and Ernest lived in Edmonton and were two years away from retirement. Their children had moved to the west coast and had brilliant careers in Vancouver. Pauline and Ernest vacationed in Vancouver each summer and had a lot of fun with their grandchildren. One evening, Pauline and Ernest received a call from Vancouver. Their daughter had found them a retirement condo—a fabulous place they could not afford to miss out on.

Caught by surprise Pauline and Ernest wondered how they best could arrange the purchase considering their pre-retirement situation. Their banker advised them that the smartest way would be to buy the condo with a credit line. As the family home of Pauline and Ernest was debt free, they could sell it when the timing was right and when they would get a great sale price for it. Once they had the money in their pockets, they could then pay down, in full, the credit line on their new condominium or keep whatever credit made economical sense to them, consolidating all debt into one.

Learn from this story: Taking out a credit line was the ideal way to finance this purchase. The couple knew they would be making a large lump sum payment to pay down this credit line as soon as they sold their debt-free house. With a credit line, any lump sum payments are free of penalty, no matter what the size. As an additional benefit, there then is the option to consolidate all household debt into the credit line, paying less interest than would be the case with a credit line not insured by real estate—or with a credit card. Once the credit line is partially paid down, the credit can be taken out again any time for other types of purchases without the need for renewed negotiations with the bank.

Pre-approved Mortgages

Having pre-approved financing in place is a great way to start the search for your home or investment property. It will put you in a much better position against any competing offer. When your real estate agent can present an offer on your behalf with pre-approved financing, your offer carries more weight than a competing offer that is "subject to financing." The seller might accept your offer right away because the funds are there and the offer is not going to fall through. Depending on the seller's personality, you could be spared a bidding war if another person presents an offer at the same time.

Here is the process: According to your list of needs, you know the type of house you are searching for and your affordability study tells you how much you are willing to spend. Taking into account the funds you have available, you'll know how much you need to borrow. It is now time to see your banker and specify the maximum amount you would like to borrow. The bank will give you a questionnaire to gather information to use in an assessment of your financial situation. Pretty soon the bank will let you know how much credit or the size of the mortgage they will approve for you. Ask for the best rate. The bank then will lock that rate in for you for the following 120 days. However, be sure to get your pre-approved financing in writing so you can have proof and backup of your pre-approved financing whenever you need it.

With your financing in place, the hunt is on for the best deal in your preferred neighbourhood. Be aware that the exact amount of financing your bank will ultimately extend to you depends to a great extent on the bank's own appraisal of the specific property you want to purchase.

If it takes some time for you to find the ideal property, and interest rates go up, you have your rate reserved. If rates decline, the bank will allow you the current lower rate when you are ready to sign your mortgage documents. If for any reason your search takes longer than 120 days, just apply for another pre-approved financing package.

However, if you have set your sights on a project where the completion may be twelve or even twenty-four months away, your bank may be able to provide you with a pre-approved mortgage that will hold a rate for up to twenty-four months. Again, if rates subsequently decline, you may be eligible to borrow at a lower rate when you finally make your purchase.

If you feel comfortable dealing with more than one financial institution, it is wise to compare terms and rates. There are various products on the market and you'll learn which one is best suited for your personal needs. Banks compete with each other for your business and, on top of a variety of products, rates will differ too. Your own bank may give you preferential treatment and a better rate than their official rate, yet the competition might offer a still lower rate and better terms.

Not everybody can produce a first-grade credit check. If somewhere down the road you were not so lucky and your credit rating took a beating, your best bet is probably to see a mortgage broker. A mortgage broker deals with many different banks and even private investors, and here you have a better chance of being approved as a customer. Furthermore, a mortgage broker will try to find you the best rate among all the offers out there in the marketplace. To illustrate, here is Rodger's story:

Rodger's Story

Rodger had never owned his own place or any property. Then came the day when, in the booming Alberta economy (annual growth rate for 2006 was 6.8 per cent*), his old apartment block fell victim to the construction of a prestigious large condo complex marketed with high-profile advertising. With a close to zero vacancy rate in the rental market of his home town of Calgary (0.5 per cent as reported on June 6, 2007*), Rodger's best friend advised him to go and see a real estate agent with the notion of becoming a home owner instead of wasting any more time in the search for new rental accommodation. To be helpful, his friend arranged an appointment for Rodger with his own real estate agent.

After they had put together a loose framework of Rodger's ideas, this real estate agent suggested he should see a mortgage broker. Also, he explained to Rodger that he should become pre-approved for a certain amount of financing so that his offer on a property would be much stronger and give him more bargaining power.

Off he went to see a mortgage broker. There Rodger's learning experience was pushed further. Suddenly the competition in mortgage rates between the different institutions made sense to him. He had a choice between two lenders, both of whom offered attractive rates. After a bit of pondering, he chose the lender who offered him the bigger prepayment option with no penalty—20 per cent per year. If he decided to resell his home, he would pay a closing penalty on only 80 per cent of the mortgage after the first year, on 60 per cent of the mortgage after the second year, and so forth.

*Statistical source: Canada Mortgage and Housing—Edmonton Rental Market Report, June 6, 2007.[xiv]

Learn from this story: Rodger's story shows that it is absolutely worthwhile to go shopping among different lenders because their products vary. A mortgage broker can easily facilitate this.

Reverse Mortgages

You paid off your mortgage long ago. As you get older, you decide there are things to do—actually dreams you always thought about, yet never had the time or means to fulfill. Now, taking money out against your home may give you that freedom and would make perfect sense. This is the idea behind a reverse mortgage. You may want to buy a new car, go on a Caribbean cruise, or help your adult children pay for their university education. Of course, the idea of a reverse mortgage could also apply if you were not so healthy anymore and could afford greater comfort with some minor changes in form of renovations, for example, to your kitchen or bathroom. With a reverse mortgage you can stay living in your house. You might even increase your equity if you modernize your house.

Reverse mortgages are intended for seniors. How much cash you can take out on a reverse mortgage can depend on the current value of your home, whether the home is mortgage free or close to mortgage free, the level of interest rates, and your age. In general, the greater the value of your home, and therefore the higher the equity you have built up in your home, the greater the amount the bank will lend you.

As long as you live in your home and it is your principal residence, you don't need to pay back any of the funds you receive through a reverse mortgage. The drawback of using a reverse mortgage comes only when you sell your home. At that time, you or your beneficiaries need to pay back the money received through the reverse mortgage, with all applicable fees and interest payments added to the originally borrowed amount.

Conclusion

When choosing among different financing options, you need to ask yourself some basic questions:

- How much of a down payment can I afford?
- Where do I think interest rates are heading in the future?
- Am I adverse to interest rate risk?
- How often and how quickly can I pay down my mortgage?
- Am I going to make prepayments?
- Can I afford higher monthly premiums or am I in need of lower monthly premiums?
- Would I like to pay interest only?
- Do I need financing insurance?
- Do I want to take money out of my home equity?
- Do I want to consolidate my household debt at a lower interest rate?

To help you in the complex decision making process, talk to a banker or mortgage broker. If you have followed the advice in this book all along and have already established a solid business relation with your own personal banker, go and seek his or her advice.

> ### Key Points
>
> ❖ Understand different types of mortgages/ credit lines.
> ❖ Decide on type of mortgage right for you.
> ❖ Compare rates and terms among lenders.
> ❖ Get pre-approved financing.
> ❖ Establish a business relationship with a personal banker.
> ❖ Decide if you need mortgage/credit line insurance.

Chapter 8:

The Search for Property

Every year in spring, the supply of all different types of real estate suddenly increases dramatically. The "for sale" signs on lawns are in competition with the spring flowers, and buyers and sellers have high hopes and bustle with activity. During the long, dark, and cold winter you had enough time to conceptualize your dream home and come to the decision that you will move to greener pastures. How should you plan this? Let us look at the various ways to search for the right property.

On the Internet

There is no difference really if you are in the market for your dream home or an investment property or a retirement condo. These days, the most efficient method for finding out what is available on the market is to search on the Internet. It is very easy to access the Multiple Listing Service (MLS) of the big cities or your home town. Simply go to www.mls.ca and click on the map of your province of interest. Then, all you need to do is to select the desired area in the province and then your city of choice. Next, point out the type of property and indicate your price range. You can then scroll through listing after listing. Soon you will get a feeling for what you can buy, and the average prices in the area of your search. If you find no listings in your target price range, you could widen your search and try the neighbouring areas. It is advisable to take some notes from the listings that spark your interest (or print them out). For the weekend, plan a drive-by tour to see for yourself how your picks impress you when you see them in real with your own eyes. If you devote some of your spare time to a thorough search, you will be able to compare pricing and spot bargains. Furthermore, you will know which properties move fast and which ones are laggards.

In the Newspaper

Browsing the real estate section of your local paper is also a promising start. In addition, in shopping malls, at banks, or in front of real estate agent's offices there are bundles of local free real estate papers. The advantage with these is that you can see all listings without limiting your search to your own criteria—as you do when searching the MLS system on the Internet. Therefore, you'll probably pick up some new ideas as to what kind of property you may like and what you don't like. For example, you might see a property you like in an area that you previously did not consider in your search, or you might you see something interesting in a slightly higher or lower price range than what you had in mind.

Open Houses

In your search for the ideal neighbourhood you spotted that lovely hillside with the gorgeous view. Or, you found a specific subdivision that you liked and imagined as your new neighbourhood. In either case, this now is the time to do more than simply look for "for sale" signs. It is a good idea to attend any open houses; they are an excellent opportunity to obtain information and to find a great value.

If you have the intention of getting into the market for the very first time, it is in your best interest to familiarize yourself with the term "open house." Ideally, you should go to many open houses, so you will no longer be intimidated by the real estate agents' professional eloquence or be overly impressed with the staging artists' superior taste. You will then no longer be detracted, but utterly focused on the minute details of the place you intend to buy.

By attending open houses, you will develop a feeling for what is attractive to you as well as for what you don't like. Analyze each open house according to your own needs and wants lists and the price you had in mind.

There are deals out there that you may not have spotted without an open house opportunity. When luck strikes and you find the right place, your buying decision will be well balanced rather than impulsive. Here is the story of Jim:

Jim's Story

Jim lived in an upscale, fairly new condo complex with about 120 units and a great variety of floor plans. One day, Jim's next-door neighbour had an open house for his condo. As Jim was in the habit of attending as many open houses as possible to get a feeling for the market, he could not refrain himself from checking out his neighbour's condo.

To his great surprise, for the next three months or so, there seemed to be an open house at his neighbour's condo just about every weekend. During these three months, Jim followed the unit's pricing development on the MLS. Within that time frame the asking price was significantly lowered. The total reduction amounted to $25,000—or around 6 per cent. Some additional research and comparisons with other units for sale in that same building showed that the asking price for this particular condo had now fallen well below market value. And then came that most significant information: while sharing the elevator to his fifth-floor condo, Jim learned from another resident of the building that the owner of the condo that was for sale was being transferred overseas and thus was eager to sell.

There was nothing wrong with the condo. It was much larger than Jim's place, and it was a south-facing unit with a full view of the park. Why not go for such a welcome upgrade for a bargain price? Jim had his real estate agent put in a low offer to see what would happen. The offer was countered with only a slight increase, and they soon agreed on a new price. The deal was excellent.

Learn from this story: Attend as many open houses as possible. You never know when an opportunity might just present itself. Follow the price movements of properties that interest you by studying the MLS on the Internet. You will get to know the market fairly well.

For Sale by Owner

It is rather important to develop a feeling for the market. Usually buyers expect a bargain if they find a place that is "for sale by owner" because the owner saves by not having to pay a real estate commission and therefore, in theory, could offer his property for less. You would also think these sellers have some expertise to be able to sell their home on their own and thus save on costs. However, experience points in the opposite direction. These properties are often overpriced and real estate agents, for ethical reasons, do not include them in their portfolios. On the other hand, don't be discouraged by a few bad apples.

Keeping this warning in mind and having a bit of market savvy will help you find a house being sold by its owner that fits your needs and expectations. Of course, it may also be your lucky day and you may find an under-priced property for which the seller has misjudged the fair market value.

Presentation Centers

It can be great fun to visit presentation centers. If your idea is to check out some recently opened presentation centers for new building projects, you might find locations, floor plans, and designs that are really hot and interesting. You then should review the floor plans and matching price lists at home with a sharp pencil and a calculator, and compare the various projects.

If the construction of the units has already reached a stage where you are able to walk through, you may spot a unit for which the price has not yet been adjusted for things that are particularly attractive, like larger or wrap-around balconies in lower units compared to the higher floors, or partial nice views, or some other features. Just to give you an example: it could be that, once you have reached the third floor, the rooftops of neighbouring houses are below eyelevel, thus allowing for some view, while the builder is asking for premium prices only from the fourth floor up.

Or, if the sales brochure praises the fairy-tale setting of the wonderful new development, especially pointing out fantastic views, then everybody's expectation level will be sky high. Here, you might zoom in on first- and second-floor levels, which may have no view at all and, consequently, will hold no interest from buyers who came to buy view properties on the higher levels. In this instance, you may encounter reasonably priced condos in a luxury environment. The astute investor will use these price variations within a building to his or her advantage.

For an example of how a buyer can spot an undervalued unit within a new condominium building, here is the story of Jane:

Jane's Story

Jane drove to a presentation center in the suburbs. The project was a brand-new, four-floor condominium building with fifty-five units. At the display center Jane took her time to study the floor plans, taking into account the floor level, the size, and the price of each unit. She liked the display model, so she asked for a tour of the building, which was not yet quite finished. Wearing a hardhat and accompanied by a sales person, she was given a walk-through. They took the stairs and, floor by floor, they looked at various units.

When she entered a south-facing unit on the fourth floor, not only was Jane impressed by the beautiful, open view and even distant mountain view from the living room and balcony, but she also noticed the high vaulted ceiling featured in the living room/dining room combination. The equivalent unit on the third floor naturally did not have vaulted ceilings, nor was the view as pristine. Yet, the price difference between the equivalent third floor-unit and this top-floor unit was only $4,000! In theory, the price difference between the third-floor unit and the top-floor unit with vaulted ceilings should be somewhere between $15,000 and $20,000. Jane knew that there was a distinctive market for top-floor condos as some people only consider buying top-floor condominiums as their home. There is a certain prestige attached to top floor condos—no one walks above you!

To make sure that she had found a great deal for that top floor unit, Jane had to know if the entire development was well priced in comparison to other projects with about the same building standard. As this was the case, Jane returned the next day to sign a contract of purchase for the top-floor unit and pay the down payment required. What a great deal!

Learn form this story: When pricing new developments, builders approximate values to their theoretical vision of the finished building. Detailed, careful inspection of the units, in combination with a thorough analysis of the price list, helps the sophisticated investor spot comparatively undervalued units once construction is in progress or near completion.

The Buyer's Real Estate Agent

At some point, your preliminary checklist will be completed and you will know exactly what is right for you. You have a financial framework and you will have decided to buy a house, a condo, or a townhouse—old or new—and you know the neighbourhood where you think you would fit in and be happy. This, of course, could be the right time for you to have a real estate agent involved in the search. Now that you can give a detailed description of what you are looking for, you are the ideal client. It is important to communicate your priorities in detail.

Having a real estate agent assist you in your search could be rather beneficial. Yet, if you still discover properties on your own and develop a keen interest, have your real estate agent make the appointments so that you can view them together. Of course, your real estate agent will also show you properties that fill only one or two of your criteria, and don't really match your expectations. Never feel pressured to buy anything you are not totally satisfied with. It does not matter if you have viewed twenty-something places or have been looking for several months. If you are not sure, don't buy!

The buyer's real estate agent will be discussed in more detail in Chapter 10.

Conclusion

The more actively you search for you ideal home or investment property, and the more time and effort you invest in your search, the greater are the chances you will be successful, both financially and in fulfilling your dreams. The broader your search, the more likely you will find that real gem. When looking for your new home, or that great deal on an investment property, with lots of potential of upwards appreciation and an overall good return on your money, all your efforts to acquire a good knowledge of the subject will be greatly rewarded.

Don't restrict your search to just one search medium, or you may never hear about the great property advertised elsewhere. Combine your efforts with the efforts of a real estate agent and you will be a step ahead in finding the best possible property for your specific needs and wishes. But also, invest your own time and energy and do your own research. Don't solely rely on your real estate agent's search. Only you know best which property fits all your criteria and interests you the most. And, there is the little-known fact that most real estate agents may not show you properties that are listed with discount commission agencies, as they would earn very little in commission, and, of course, they will not show you those that are "for sale by owner."

Key Points

- Your search for good valued properties:
  - ❖ Research the MLS on the Internet.
  - ❖ Browse through the weekly real estate paper.
  - ❖ Read the real estate section of the local newspaper.
  - ❖ On the weekend, attend open houses.
  - ❖ Look for "for sale" signs on lawns.
  - ❖ Check out developers' presentation centers.

- Let your own buyer's real estate agent help you in the search.

Chapter 9:

Risk Management

In this chapter we'll be talking about house inspections, insurance, warranties, and general risk factors you face when you buy properties, whether old or new. This chapter deals with those things that, at first glance, seem trivial, but, if you are not prepared, may cause you nasty surprises.

Worst of all, these surprises can prove to be very costly and could have catastrophic consequences for your pocketbook and your budget. Not knowing how to handle the risks listed in this chapter could also cost you the approval for financing by your lender. For example, few banks would be willing to provide financing for a leaky condo (as will be explained later in this chapter).

House Inspections

There are many reasons that attracted you to a specific property and prompted you to consider buying it. But, as you know, good looks can be deceiving. It is of the utmost importance that the property is also safe and sound.

New construction comes with warranties. When you buy new construction, you have one big advantage: there are extensive warranties to cover the building. By law, builders must provide a third-party, 2-5-10-year warranty that covers any structural defects for a period of ten years. This warranty also includes a five-year building envelope warranty and two-year coverage for any defect in materials and labour in the electrical, plumbing, heating, ventilation, and air conditioning systems, as well as the exterior cladding, caulking, windows, and doors. Some builders now offer a 2-10-10 warranty. In addition, any new construction integrates the latest earthquake-resistant building technology. If you have set your sights on a remediated condo on the west coast of British Columbia, the new rainscreen technology also comes with a long warranty (rainscreen exterior walls keep rain from getting to inside walls).

But, if you are interested in buying a unit from someone other than the developer, or a unit where warranties are no longer applicable, you need to have an inspection by a professional inspector before you buy. It is important to have this inspection for any type of building—be it a house, condo, or townhouse. Your purchase and sales contract needs to include a "subject to house inspection" clause.

As an example, your building inspector could discover that the wiring of a character home—an older home built in the first decades of the last century with heritage value—is not up to safety standards. If you decide to go ahead with the purchase nevertheless, you could try to get a deduction from the purchase price to offset the additional estimated costs of an upgrade bill. To have a building inspector go through the project may cost a few hundred dollars, but, in the final analysis, you might save a lot of money when renegotiating your offer. Or, you could walk away from a prospective deal and avoid having any more nasty surprises in the future.

If the building inspection becomes part of the deal, before that deal is finalized, the inspector will give you a complete report, and will explain all of the shortcomings to you in person after he has carefully examined the property. He will also provide cost estimates for the repairs for which you can then budget properly and according to a pre-set time schedule.

The story will be different if your building inspector warns you about termites or carpenter ants, rodent infestations, or if essential wooden supports are rotting or contaminated with fungi. More often than not, buyers just don't want to deal with these kinds of problems, yet the untrained eye might not even notice the damage. That is why it pays to work with an experienced inspector.

Always be wary when buying a house where add-ons by the previous owner never passed general building regulations. Major safety concerns may become an issue here. Any house you are interested in making an offer on should comply with building codes. Self-styled basement suites, interior walls that have been taken out to create larger spaces, decks that were built on a shoestring budget are all dangers to your safety and that of your loved ones. The risks involved are simply not worth it.

Insurance

Now that the "subject to building inspection" clause can be taken out of your purchasing contract, and you are happy that your future house, townhouse, or condo is free of any major problems, you must think about insurance for the new property. Insurance should start with the completion date of your contract of purchase and sale. Insurance companies will advise you on which is the best over-all coverage you can buy in your particular situation. The insurance company will offer you premiums that can be lowered by raising the deductibles. You also qualify for lower premiums if you have not filed any claims in the past, if you are a senior, or if your home is monitored by an alarm system.

If you set your sights on an older property, be aware that you may have to do some shopping around to find an insurance company eager to insure your property. Insurance companies are risk adverse and shy away from homes where the foundations, the electrical wiring, and/or the heating systems do not comply with today's building codes or standards. If you do find an insurance company that offers you coverage, expect the premiums to be significantly higher than they would be for a comparable new house.

It is important to be insured for the adequate amount at all times. Never be underinsured in order to save money. With rising property values, most people frown as their tax assessments increase year after year, but they simply don't follow through on protecting their properties adequately by adjusting their insurance coverage to the new market value of the insured property. Without knowing it, these homeowners become underinsured. In a red-hot market, insured values have to be adjusted to market values every single year. You must be insured for the full replacement cost of your house. It is best to ask a professional appraiser or your real estate agent for a precise market evaluation of all your properties.

Julia and Sam's Story

Julia and Sam unfortunately lost their house due to a fire. Though desperate, they thought their insurance would cover the loss of their home. When they went to their insurance company, they discovered that the insurance payout was by no means adequate to cover the replacement cost of their house. They had last revised their insurance policy many years ago and were consequently severely underinsured. All of the expensive renovations they had undertaken in their house over the previous year turned out to be lost money. They simply could not comprehend such terrible loss.

Learn from this story: Whatever renovations you have done in your house, be it a new roof, new windows, new flooring, or remodeling the kitchen or bathroom, remember that all these additions increase the value of your house and it is entirely at your peril not to adjust your insurance coverage accordingly.

If you live in an earthquake zone like the Pacific Rim, it is highly recommended that you purchase earthquake insurance. It is the strata council who makes the decision to buy earthquake insurance for a townhouse or condominium complex—and how much to buy. Therefore, don't assume that proper coverage is in place. It is of the utmost importance that you ask your strata council if the building is adequately insured. Earthquake insurance usually comes with a very high deductible, such as 10 per cent. Ideally, it should cover replacement costs, but sometimes it covers only a fraction of building's value. This makes it all the more important that insurance payments by the strata are annually adjusted to reflect the latest increases in the market value of the building. As condo owner and occupier, you can also purchase additional earthquake insurance for your specific unit to cover potential losses of your personal contents in the event of an earthquake.

When you are at your lawyer's office signing your purchase documents, your lawyer will ask you if you wish to purchase title insurance for your new property. You may be looking at a cost of roughly $150 to $250 to do so. Unless you finance your purchase to the maximum and are planning to keep it that way for the years to come, it is a smart idea to purchase title insurance to protect the equity you have tied up in your new property now or in the future. Title insurance protects the equity you have in your new property from "real estate thieves." Can West News Service published an article in the *Times Colonist* on March 16, 2007, written by Mario Toneguzzi, who writes, "Scams are estimated to cost Canadians up to $1.5 billion yearly," and "… scams often average as much as $300,000 per case …"[xv]

Real estate scams in Canada are on the rise. There are "real estate thieves" who, using fake identification, actually succeed in taking out crooked mortgages on properties that don't belong to them. When you have purchased title insurance, as long as you own your property, it cannot be transferred criminally into someone else's name. Title insurance also protects you if there are defects in the title, unpaid liens, zoning problems with your new property, or costs that can surface from violations to the building code.

The Leaky Condo Syndrome on BC's West Coast

As every senior real estate agent will tell you, condo owners and construction companies on the west coast of Canada had major headaches in the mid-1980s and throughout the 1990s. Aptly called "the leaky condo syndrome," the problem spread like a disease and caught many people totally by surprise. Condo owners lost tens of thousands of dollars, and condominium buildings with the syndrome became taboo—people would not touch them for fear of further losses.

Basically, the condo market collapsed. As these condos affected by the leaky condo syndrome will still be with us for the foreseeable future—some are now on the market as "remediated" condos—it is essential for the buyer on the west coast to be knowledgeable on this subject.

The West Coast "Leaky Condo Syndrome" Story

In the 1980s, some construction requirements of condominium buildings and townhouses on the rainy and damp west coast of British Columbia changed in accordance with a change in the building code. A synthetic stucco was introduced to be used as the exterior envelope of new construction. The problem arose because this stucco did not "breathe"—did not let air in or out. The overhangs of the new buildings were not large or long enough to turn away the rain and moisture from heavy downpours. Moisture became trapped behind the stucco, leading to rotten wood frames, rotten and moldy insulation materials, and rusty steel frames. Herewith, the "leaky condo syndrome" was born. Many people were devastated when their beautiful new strata units suffered extensive building envelope damage, which resulted in equal damage to people's pocketbooks. Condo and townhouse prices took a nosedive.

How to remedy the situation? Rainscreen technology came on the market. Moisture-related problems are not easily fixed. The remediation process is very expensive. The building envelope of the damaged buildings must be completely stripped and redone with rainscreen technology. You can tell when these building are in the phase of remediation because exterior walls are wrapped in covers from top to bottom. This is the process the buildings undergo before they reappear for sale with the words: building fully remediated.

Today, some formerly leaky buildings have been remediated, but many have not. Buyer beware! There are still many rumours going around in the marketplace as to which buildings may be leaky buildings. Your real estate agent may also be able to help you with identifying a leaky building. As a matter of fact, many townhouses built between 1985 and 2000 also have the same exterior synthetic stucco as the leaky condos do, and, at the present time, most of these buildings have not undergone any remediation or have only undergone a partial remediation. They could therefore, in the future, easily become leaky townhouses. A safer bet when buying a townhouse built during this time would be to look for one with wood or simulated wood siding rather than stucco siding, as wood siding and look-alikes generally allow buildings to breathe, meaning that mold and rot is less of a problem.

So, would a remediated building be a good buy? To pay for the rather expensive process of remediation, strata councils had to struggle to come up with the financing. If the strata decided to pay in a reasonably short time for the remediation, special assessments for the owners were established. Leaky condo owners suffered tremendous financial losses. However, in many cases, the strata fees shot up sky-high, and some strata councils instituted mortgage-like payment plans. For you, today's buyer, this means you should have a close look at those strata fees and also at the minutes of past strata meetings before you come to any buying decision. There have been individual and class action lawsuits, and some are still pending, but many leaky condo owners paid out of pocket for the damage and have never been properly reimbursed. Even when a leaky condo lawsuit is won, the reimbursement to the owners usually covers only a certain percentage of the costs involved in the remediation of the building.

When you are in the market and consider buying into a building with stucco exterior, make a mental note that condo buildings and townhouses built in the 1990s on BC's west coast almost exclusively used synthetic stucco. If you see dark water stains or green mold on the exterior stucco, you are most likely looking at a building with synthetic stucco. Also, ask your building inspector for an exterior inspection of the building in addition to an inspection of your unit. Mention the leaky condo syndrome to the inspector. If your condo fits under this heading, the inspector will show you what has been done or what still needs to be done and what the costs will be.

"Rainscreen" technology

Today's new construction of condominium and townhouse complexes in British Columbia uses rainscreen technology right from the start to fit in with the west coast weather condition. In the case of rainscreen technology, a capillary break separates the exterior cladding of a building from the next interior sheathing. This technique prevents moisture from seeping into the frame, which guarantees that no mold will ever grow, there will be no rot, or, in the case of a concrete building, rust. The British Columbia building code has adopted changes in regard to rainscreen technology and, as of December 15, 2006, single-family homes will also have to adhere to the new standards in order to qualify for the province's new home warranty plan.

Risks in Buying Older Properties

Strata Inefficiencies

Any building in a strata, whether a condominium building, townhouse, or a single-home development, is overseen by a strata council. The strata council is at the heart of the decisions made on behalf of the complex, and also does the accounting for the strata operations. If you are buying into an existing complex, your contract of purchase should include the clause "subject to viewing the strata minutes, the strata bylaws, and the financial statements." It is of utmost importance for you to know what is going on in the strata and what the strata's plans are.

One look into the financial statements, the most recent operating statements, and the strata minutes tells it all. You will see any extraordinary expenses which will tell you volumes about problems within the strata complex. Problems that are anticipated, yet not budgeted for, will appear as resolutions in those minutes. Common concerns are leaky roofs, older balconies, leaky underground parking, leaky swimming pools, and elevators and hot water tanks in need of maintenance. All of these issues are discussed by the strata council members. When you buy your condo, you will be invited to take part in these meetings and encouraged to vote on all major activities within the strata. When you make your purchase decision, find out the amount of your monthly strata fees, but also find out if there are adequate reserves in the contingency fund, and if repairs are properly budgeted for. When you see a lot of "for sale" signs popping up at the same time in a strata, you might suspect that there are some special issues that must be dealt with, and it is in your best interest to find out what it is all about.

Termites and Mold

Termites are the most common problem in older housing in areas that were formerly part of large forests. Again, it is wise to involve a building inspector. Simply walking through the house yourself and having a look around will not be a good enough guarantee that there is no termite damage. The inspector knows where to look for structural damage. Even if the house owner hired pest control specialists or fumigated himself shortly before putting his place on the market, the building inspector will notice the telltale signs. Inner city buildings can be infested with different bugs—like silverfish, for example.

In older, poorly ventilated housing, a thorough inspection by a professional is recommended to test for the presence of molds. Molds like to grow in humid, moist, and poorly aired places, such as damp basements, or in bathrooms and kitchens with leaking sinks and fans that don't work. Molds generate spores which are unhealthy for humans and are a risk to you if they exist inside your home. When you live in a home that harbors molds, you may not see them right away, as they may grow underneath the carpet or behind the walls, but you could suffer from allergy-like symptoms such as sneezing, runny nose, watery eyes, a persistent cough, or even migraine headaches. You definitely don't want to buy a house or condominium where molds are present. However, if you have already fallen in love with such a home, find out how the situation can be rectified and how much this would cost before you sign the contract of purchase and sale.

When employing a real estate agent to sell a property, the owner must disclose any major problems such as termites or molds in the property disclosure statement. However, the seller may not even know that molds are present in the home. Just to be on the safe side, listen to your building inspector and analyze the report rather critically.

Risks when Buying New Properties

You may think that buying into a brand-new development is risk free—this is not the case. The sales centers of brand-new developments now open their doors prior to even any work starting on the construction site and there are cases where units are sold an entire year or more in advance of any construction start. If you are buying in the pre-construction phase there are two major risks: building delays and cost-cutting by the builders.

- *Building delays.* Your building's construction may be delayed because there are financial problems—units might not sell well or the developer may not able to find or pay the subcontracting because of material and labour shortages. When real estate markets reach the top of the cycle, the usually robust system gets fragile. If a bidding war occurs about cement and steel rods, or the prices for items such as drywall, siding, and heating shoot up, the pre-construction price structure for the project might get squeezed and new financing has to be secured. In this case, time works against the developer. He may get stuck and, for a while, your down payment will be stuck too.

  Even when there is progress in the construction, the completion date of your contract may be further and further advanced because of countless delays attributable to the building boom. When lots of builders want windows, carpets, doors, and cabinets at the same time, there is a system overload. Perhaps you sold your old home for a terrific price, setting the completion date two months in advance to match the completion date of the purchase contract of your new condo. In theory, you could have moved smoothly from your old house into your new condo. The problem comes when construction of the new condo is delayed and you do not receive the keys until three months after the completion date of the sale of your old house. In the meantime, you need a place to stay and a place to store your furniture. This will cost you extra trouble, extra money, and double the moving expenses.

There is yet a greater risk: you have signed to buy the condo and have made a down payment between 5 and 50 per cent of the purchase price. After one full year, the developer finally quits and does not proceed with the planned construction for any number of reasons. You receive your deposit back and are in a position to sue for interest. As one year has passed, the problem is that prices for a comparable unit are now much higher. You have therefore missed out on the appreciation of the unit you bought, and, if you buy another unit in today's market conditions, you will be paying a higher price.

• *Cost-cutting by the builders.* As construction costs skyrocket and there is a market plateau on the price for which a developer can sell new units, developers in collaboration with builders may be looking to build cheaper so that they can still make the profit they were hoping for. The new trend in construction is to offer less square footage and possibly reduced interior decoration quality for the same price, downsizing from 1000-square-foot, two-bedroom units to smaller, 750-square-foot, two-bedroom units; building 450-square-foot studios in lieu of 700-square-foot, one-bedroom units; eliminating extra amenities such as storage lockers or bike rooms; replacing walk-in closets with smaller, regular closets; replacing larger bathrooms with tiny ones; downgrading the quality of the flooring with cheaper options; installing cheap plastic bathtubs and showers—and on and on. A similar tendency can be seen in new single-family housing projects. Building lots of only 4,000 square feet are now offered in brand-new subdivisions, and houses are built on two or three levels to minimize the amount of land used. In any case, the luxury we once took for granted now comes at a much higher price, and affordability becomes an issue.

Despite these pitfalls and dangers, the real estate market for new construction is still humming and buzzing, and ads are as enticing as ever. To compensate for the old luxury, the new urban lifestyle becomes well propagated and the thrill of superb marketing keeps us happily fascinated with how great our opportunities are. And, indeed, there are opportunities at all times. But be selective. It is one thing to be impressed by superb marketing. Yet we are in a completely different category and you had better be very careful when life savings are at stake and a respectably sized, two-bedroom-plus-den condo with some views goes for the price of nearly half a million dollars.

Conclusion

If you are in the market to buy a strata property or condo in the pre-construction phase, you are well advised to take the time to enquire if the developer did finish his previous projects to the full satisfaction of his customers. Moreover, in a hot market, ask if the current project will be built absolutely to plan and on schedule.

But no matter what you are buying, you invest such a large sum of money that you want to make absolutely sure you are insured for any conceivable risk. Here the best advice is to invest enough time into the project you intend to buy, and double check every aspect, so you will not have buyer's remorse syndrome the day after.

Key Points

- Hire a professional house inspector. Beware of:
  - ❖ leaky condos/townhouses
  - ❖ handyman add-ons
  - ❖ unsafe foundations, wiring, plumbing
  - ❖ termites and molds

- Reassess your insurance coverage:
  - ❖ Do you have title insurance?
  - ❖ Is your property insured for the full replacement value?
  - ❖ Have you bought earthquake insurance?

- Prior to the purchase of a strata property, read the rules and regulations, the strata minutes and financial statements.

- Know the risks associated with buying in the pre-construction phase.

Chapter 10:

The Buyer's Real Estate Agent

Most people know that, during the process of buying or selling of real estate, a real estate agent is usually involved. So it may come as a surprise to you that there are a lot of differentiations you can play out to your advantage—actually there is the seller's real estate agent, the so called "listing agent", and there is in many cases the buyer's own real estate agent, the so called "buyer's agent".

Working with the Listing Real Estate Agent

When looking to buy a property, you may think the easiest way to make contact is to phone up the real estate agent who is listing the property for sale. This would be the listing real estate agent. His name and phone number, as well as his company's name, are easily taken from the "for sale" sign on the lawn or the Internet listing or the ad in the paper. In certain circumstances this might be the most practical and most efficient way to buy a property, as will be demonstrated in Diana's story.

Diana's Story

Diana had been a cosmopolitan traveler for most of her life. Her job had taken her to many places around the world and she had now decided to settle down. Her elderly parents invited her to spend her spring vacation with them in the lakeside town in which she had grown up.

How things had changed! There were new subdivisions, a school, and a pub; the former solitude was all but memory. As she was driving around the lake with her parents, a new development featuring townhouses with lake access attracted Diana's attention. Soft slopes were shaded by oak trees. Water lilies and swans made for enchanted scenery. "How serene," she thought. Diana was thrilled by her discovery and was tempted to phone the listing real estate agent immediately using her cell phone. Her parents encouraged her to do just that. Diana was lucky—the listing real estate agent was in the office and was available to show the townhouse. So she drove her parents home, and then headed out again for the appointment with the listing agent.

By the time the colour of the lake was changing to soft pastel and the sun was setting, Diana was the new owner of that townhouse. Now Diana would know where to ship a few items she wanted to keep as souvenirs from her foreign travels, together with some furniture that also had sentimental value. Diana's parents could keep an eye on things until her foreign obligations came to an end in three or four months down the road. Money was not an issue to Diana and, when the listing agent had shown her the townhouse, Diana accepted the asking price in full—not because it was a super deal, but because the townhouse was a jewel. Diana was very happy with this wonderful property so close to her parents' place.

Learn from this story: In Diana's case, time was of the essence and a sentimental attachment to the specific location had overridden any monetary issues. The townhouse was a resale and the quickest and easiest way for Diana, who was only visiting during her spring break, to buy such a property was to phone the listing agent whose sign was gracing the lawn. This agent then acted for both parties: the seller and the buyer. To avoid any legal conflict of interest between the two parties, the listing agent had to have the seller and the buyer sign a dual agency agreement. When a real estate agent acts on behalf of both parties—the buyer and the seller—the real estate agent has to be neutral. Of course, in our example, the cosmopolitan buyer also could have called on her parents' real estate agent to act as her own buyer's agent.

And, here is another example of when it may be advantageous to work with the listing real estate agent, rather than with your own buyer's real estate agent:

Julie's Story

Julie was interested in buying a condo in a 150-unit waterfront building project, which had recently been completed but was totally sold out before she knew about it. Now the re-sales were coming onto the market with many of the original investors flipping their units for profit.

Most of these investors re-listed their resale unit with the agency and the two real estate agents who originally had successfully conducted the sale of the entire project. These two real estate agents knew the project inside and out and were familiar with all the different floor plans, what the units sold for originally, and what they were selling for now. They also had a clear idea of all the features that made this project attractive to a potential buyer and why it would make a good long-term investment.

MLS listings on the Internet indicated to Julie that there were quite a few re-sales in the complex with water view, all listed with these two real estate agents. When she decided to work with these two listing agents, Julie was surprised how well they knew everything about the complex. In addition, they offered not to show other prospective buyers the unit in which Julie was interested the most, as there were other units to sell as well. So Julie would not be pressured and could take all the time to make up her mind and come to a decision she would not regret. This was really an unexpected gesture on the part of these listing real estate agents and very much appreciated. What a bonus! There would be no possibility of a competing offer or that the unit would be snatched away in front of Julie's eyes as she was negotiating the final price. These two listing agents were very upfront with Julie and told her that they wanted to earn both the seller's and the buyer's commission and therefore gave her preference before other customers brought through by other real estate agents.

So Julie took her time in negotiating a good deal on the unit she really liked.

Learn from this story: As you can see from Julie's story, there are times when it is more beneficial to work with the listing real estate agent than to bring in your own buyer's real estate agent. Then again, there are other times when it is to your advantage to work with your own buyer's real estate agent.

Your Own Buyer's Real Estate Agent

Working with your own buyer's real estate agent may become essential in a hot market. Your real estate agent gets to know each property that is listed on the Internet on a special system that can be viewed by real estate agents only. This information is available to real estate agents a few days before the public gets to see the information on the MLS. If you are able to communicate your needs and expectations accurately, your agent can set you up on the Internet so that you see all the properties that fit your description the moment they are listed with a real estate agency—and days before the public gets to see them on the MLS. This is called Private Client Service. This in itself is a huge advantage. You can be ahead of other buyers in making an offer on a property. However, it goes without saying that, often during the first days a property is listed, the seller is willing to accept only offers close to the asking price.

On the other hand, if you are in no hurry and find a property that has been on the market for a while—say in November or December when market activity can be sluggish—you may have a much better chance for a price reduction. So you will work out an offer with your own agent. The services of your own buyer's real estate agent who is also a great negotiator will always be beneficial, and you may call on that agent again and again for future transactions.

When you are satisfied with an agent, and have established a good business relationship, your agent will know your business style and your personal circumstances and will be eager to adjust to your needs with skilled negotiations. Working with your own buyer's real estate agent could prevent you from falling victim to a speculator, which is what nearly happened to Edward:

Edward's Story

Edward found on the MLS a rural acreage that attracted his attention. The property's asking price was $150,000. Upon Edward's request, his real estate agent provided him with a printout of the historic transactions of the property. It turned out that the property had been bought by the seller a month earlier for $100,000 and this new owner was trying to make a quick profit. Since purchasing the land, he had sent through a bulldozer to put in a rough driveway and to clear some trees in order to have a building site wide enough for a future house.

So, the asking price was not fair. Edward did not buy this rural acreage. By working diligently with his own buyer's realtor, Edward avoided falling victim to a speculator.

Learn from this story: Your buyer's real estate agent can provide you with valuable information. In essence, your own buyer's real estate agent will work specifically for you, representing your interests when negotiating with the seller. There is a lot of information your buyer's real estate agent can give you on the property in which you are interested. Here is a short checklist of what you could ask your own buyer's real estate agent:

- *A comparative market analysis.* This analysis shows you the approximate market value of the property you are interested in purchasing. Your buyer's real estate agent will also show you comparative properties so that you can see for yourself.

- *The number of days the property has been on the market.* This knowledge helps to better estimate your chances when putting in a lower offer instead of accepting to pay full price. The longer the property has been on the market, the more likely a lowball offer will be accepted by the seller. Your low offer may also make sense from a different point of view: if the property has been sitting on the market for some time, there is less chance that competing offers will drive up the sales price or put you in danger of missing out on the project. Here your agent also would tell you if there had been offers on the property that had been rejected by the owner.

• *Figures for the tax assessment value of the property.* Your agent can provide you with figures for both the land value and the building improvement value and the taxes paid in the previous year on the property. You can then look at the tax assessment value of comparable properties and see what the asking price is for them. This again can give you an idea of the fair market value of the property you are thinking about buying.

• *The price the seller originally paid for the property and how long ago it was purchased.* This will give you an insight into the amount of profit the seller is trying to achieve and the timeframe in which he is trying to do so. If the profit seems unreasonable, you may have a closer look at what the fair market value of the property in today's market really is, so you can make an informed decision when working out your offer.

Ask your real estate agent these questions and use the information to your advantage.

Finding a Good Buyer's Real Estate Agent

Your buyer's real estate agent should be an excellent negotiator, and you must like his or her personal style. Before any deal is reached, it is your agent who negotiates on your behalf to align your offer with the conditions of the seller in order to come to an agreement for all the conditions of the sale. You want to pay the lowest possible price on any real estate purchase you make, and you want the agent to be available any time you need him or her. So, if your agent knows your background, motivations, and skills, and knows your personal banker, this knowledge certainly would speed up any action and ideally would make both of you more successful in your common dealings.

However, where do you start if this is your first real estate investment? How do you find a good real estate agent? One obvious way is by word of mouth through friends, neighbours, or work colleagues. If you are new to a town, you could also look at the agents' awards page in the local newspaper. Larger real estate offices periodically publish the names of their top-producing real estate agents. However, there could be possible drawbacks to using a real estate agent who is well-known in the community; for example, a decreased level of personal attention and the delegation of your file to a subordinate. Here is Laura's story:

Laura's Story

Laura attended a real estate seminar at a hotel given by a well known local real estate agent. Laura was very impressed. The real estate agent gave tips on real estate investing and made everything look so easy. The man was charmingly eloquent and had a rather persuading style, so Laura listened carefully and, after a while, she decided that this real estate agent should become her personal agent. He should become her buyer's real estate agent who would successfully work for her. The next day, she went to his office, had an informative appointment with him, and signed an exclusive contract to work with him and his office.

A few days later, Laura wanted to give her new real estate agent a copy of the paperwork for her pre-approved financing, exactly what she had been asked to do. She had arranged an appointment to see her new real estate agent at his office the minute she left her bank with the document in her hand. To her surprise, a secretary simply led her to the assistant real estate agent's room to take care of her concerns. The assistant real estate agent explained to Laura that he would be taking over her file. For a moment it did not seem right that Laura would not be working with the agent with whom she had signed an exclusive contract.

Though initially very irritated, good fortune was on her side, and Laura soon discovered that the assistant real estate agent was very hard working and never tired in showing her different properties. He developed a good understanding for what Laura was looking for. Over the years, this grew into a trusting business relationship and Laura liked to work with him as her buyer's real estate agent.

Learn from this story: When working with a very popular or very busy real estate agent, there is a high likelihood that one of his or her assistants will attend to your needs. For example, when you are in search of a property, an assistant will most likely be the person driving you around town to see different properties. Simply put, a busy and popular real estate agent does not have the time for this kind of work.

There is a whole list of possibilities of where you could meet your own buyer's real estate agent. Open houses, which you could attend and where you could informally chat with the real estate agent, are a good opportunity to find a real estate agent whose personal style appeals to you. Or, as you go and see other listings of interest to you during your house hunting quest, you'll meet real estate agents. Then, there are also booths at malls staffed by a rotation of real estate agents from a particular company. And, of course, you could simply walk into the office of a real estate agency and ask to speak to the real estate agent on duty.

Most real estate agents are very professional and very well trained. There is strong competition for your business. You will sense who is trying to be very helpful and who takes the time to understand your needs and objectives. During your discussions, you will soon get a feeling for how welcome and important your business is and if the agent will take good care of you.

When the real estate agent of your choice is successful in negotiating a good deal for you and all papers are signed, you are probably better off to just continue with him or her in a great working relationship, and there is no need to sign an exclusive contract of representation during any future dealings. Each transaction is different, and it is easier to have the freedom of choice. If you are happy with a professional relationship, you automatically will return to it whenever possible or appropriate. Here is the story of Dorothy to illustrate:

Dorothy's Story

Dorothy had simply been paying rent for the best part of her adult life and held no equity. All those years she had used her paycheck to diligently pay her monthly rent on time. It had not occurred to her how assets in real estate had been steadily growing over the last decade until all of the sudden she realized what great opportunities she had completely missed.

Without delay, Dorothy went to see a real estate agent. She chose to go to one of the larger real estate offices in town and, without an appointment or any further preparation, just dropped in. She told the real estate agent that she would like to invest in real estate and was looking for a home for herself. She thought that this was a clear mandate. She had no idea of what would follow. Right away the real estate agent pulled out a contract and had her sign a one-year agreement to work with him exclusively. Dorothy was hesitant to sign the contract, yet she mistakenly thought it to be industry practice.

Only later did Dorothy learn that she might have preferred the freedom to work with more than one agent and be more flexible, especially after she became motivated to check out suitable properties herself.

Learn from this story: Real estate is too important an issue to be left open to chance. Being knowledgeable definitively will pay off.

The Buyer's Real Estate Agent's Commission

There is a commission to be paid to the buyer's real estate agent upon a successful transaction. The commission of your buyer's real estate agent is usually paid by the seller.

However, if the seller listed his or her property with a discount commission realty company, the commission paid by the seller may not be enough to fully cover your buyer's real estate agent's commission. If this is the case, you, the buyer, need to step in and pay part of your buyer's real estate agent's commission. You could raise the issue at the negotiating table and try to negotiate a lower purchase price because of your increased costs.

Conclusion

You always can direct your inquiries to the listing agent. When you are house hunting away from home, your best bet is to simply phone up the listing real estate agent of a property that interests you. Equally, when you are in your home town but just passively browsing through and viewing listings, mostly to get a market overview or to make up your mind on what you are really looking for, the quickest way to get information is to phone up the listing real estate agent of the houses, townhouses, condos, or building lots that you would like to view.

Understand the difference between the information-gathering process and the actual buying or decision-making process. If you are actively searching for your new home or investment property, and are ready to buy, and have narrowed down the area and type of housing you are looking for, then you will want to involve your own buyer's agent in the search. When you are seriously considering a property, your own buyer's real estate agent will provide you with all the information and advice you need to find the best property in synchronicity with your needs and wish list, and make your purchase the best possible, both on a financial level and a logistical level—seeing it through to the end. Establishing a good business relationship with your own real estate agent is a matter of trust. It will take time to get to know the right person. Once you are happy with the services you get from that agent, success will build on success. You will continue working in this relationship in the same way you do with your personal banker to reach your goals and to make you financially successful.

Key Points

- Working with the listing real estate agent:
  - ❖ Quick
  - ❖ Easy-just phone listing agent's number
  - ❖ He or she may tell you the seller's motivations
  - ❖ Convenient when you are from out of town or this is your first initiative
- Advantages of working with you own buyer's real estate agent. Your buyer's real estate agent will:
  - ❖ Have a personal relationship with you
  - ❖ Know what kind of property you are looking for
  - ❖ Show you many properties
  - ❖ Look after your interest
  - ❖ Look up all the information on the property of interest
  - ❖ Perform a comparative market analysis
  - ❖ Advise you on your offer
  - ❖ Negotiate on you behalf
- Ways to find your own buyer's real estate agent:
  - ❖ Listing agent of a property you viewed
  - ❖ Agent at an open house
  - ❖ Referral from a real estate agents' office
  - ❖ Word of mouth
  - ❖ Agents' awards page in local newspaper
  - ❖ Agent at booth in mall
  - ❖ Agent who served you well in prior deal
- Buyer's real estate agent's commission generally paid by seller.

Chapter 11:

The Offer

Your offer is one of the most important aspects of your real estate purchase. Ultimately, your offer will decide if the deal goes through or not. This chapter gives you tips on what to consider when writing up an offer.

First you must decide how important or crucial it is that you succeed in your attempt to buy a home. The level of importance will be reflected in the amount you are willing to offer.

Then you must decide when you want to move from your present house, townhouse, or condo to a new home. You will face the dilemma of deciding which comes first: Do you first sell your old property and then put an offer on a new property? Or do you first buy into a new location and then sell your "old" property?

Making an Offer on an Older Property

Let us assume your real estate agent has been giving you a tour of properties on the market that fit your description. Now sale price numbers are swirling around in your head. You have narrowed your choice down to one particular place and now consider putting in an offer. The question is, how much? To find the answer to that question, there is a strategy that might save you a bundle: don't ask how much comparable properties are *listed* for—ask how much they have been *sold* for. Your real estate agent can provide you with this information.

Off and on, fabulous old places come on the market—houses partially overgrown by vines, mature old trees in the yard, and a spot where there once was a well-tended garden but now is an enchanting potpourri of flowering plants. How much should your offer be on such a place? Sometimes the value of the land that these old houses sit on is quite high. However, more often than not, repairs and maintenance have not been kept up. If you are enthusiastic about such a place, understand what you are getting into. Point out shaky, old chimneys, single-glass windows, attics with the poorest of insulation, and a lot of other deficiencies compared to modern standards, and ask for a price reduction on the sale price. Even if a house is only fifteen to twenty years old, the kitchen and the bathrooms may not have been renovated, and remodeling may be necessary. In addition, the carpets may need to be replaced and the walls may need a new coat of paint. Again, ask for a price reduction, pointing specifically to those issues, even if the listing real estate agent has superior interior design skills and has done a fabulous job at making the interior of the house look inviting, cozy, and attractive. Before you put in your offer, picture the interior of the house on your mind's screen without the antique furniture, oil paintings, Persian rugs, and pots of flowers that belong to the seller. Picture the house furnished according to your preferred personal style. Try to envision such images and then realistically decide where you want to set the price limit in your offer.

Making an Offer on a Unit within a New Development

With new property, most sellers will ask for the full listing price. However, there are frequent exceptions to that rule. You may have a situation where the developer just recently increased his sales prices, but lets you get away with the old price. Or, the developer of a subdivision might have a building lot left over. It might be an irregular shape or it might have a minor disadvantage compared to the other lots, and the developer may therefore accept a lower offer. Obviously, a developer might accept a lowball offer on a brand-new unit if it is finished and has been sitting on the market for some time and the developer is now hoping for a quick sale; for example, if he had sold all other units and this one is the last one left. When buying brand-new, always ask if offers below the asking price are accepted.

With a brand-new development, you know that within that project there will be a certain price equilibrium because everybody buying into the project will pay approximately the same fair price adjusted to each particular unit. Yet, when the developer has sold all units and some time later the private resales come up, you can never be sure if such an individual sale is fairly priced, extremely overpriced, or an absolute bargain. This will depend on the personal circumstances of the specific seller. Before you put in an offer, ask your buyer's real estate agent for a comparative market analysis. If the property is overpriced, adjust your offer to fair market value. If the seller does not accept the offer, you had better walk away. There will be better opportunities.

Bidding

In bidding, the final purchase price may not be the only and most important factor. You also might outsmart the competition with superior "subject to" clauses, a higher deposit, or a more attractive completion date. If there is no risk of competing offers or a "price war," you can always bid less than full price. If the seller insists on full price, he or she will let you know by presenting a counteroffer at full price. Your weapon may lie in the instructions you give to your real estate agent to let the seller know that you are also looking at and considering other properties. On the other hand, if your offer is too low and considered unfair by the seller, the seller may not enter negotiations with you and come back at full price. So, generally, it may be better to present a fair offer from the start if you are really interested in buying the property. A fair offer is usually your best bet, and, in case you finally find the perfect home or splendid investment opportunity, you may want to consider offering full price. Unless a competing offer comes in, the property will most likely be yours. Bidding against time most often occurs in a hot market condition, when demand greatly exceeds supply. It may be that the real estate agent of the selling party gives you a mere two hours to decide on an offer, or it may simply be that competing offers pop up on a daily basis.

At any rate, when you find your dream home or ideal investment opportunity, act fast! Delaying your offer for a day or even an hour may cost you the deal. Here is Warren's story:

Warren's Story

At 4 PM, Warren arrived at the developer's presentation center. He became fascinated with the plans of a brand-new house—a beautiful west coast rancher style home. He could easily picture himself living in it for many years to come! Moreover, it fit his budget nicely and the size of the home and the layout was exactly what he was looking for. He also liked the location and the neighbourhood of the development.

Warren still was undecided, so he drove home. That same evening, after pondering for a few hours, Warren phoned the developer's agent and bought his future home. Though he had acted fast, he never regretted this move.

When Warren met the agent the next morning to sign the paperwork, the agent confided to him that it had been Warren's fast grip of the situation that had saved him from a bidding war. That very evening another investor had also spotted the opportunity and had wanted to buy Warren's new house.

Learn from this story: Most often people have to live with their decisions for years to come. If you find a house that is ideal for you, act fast. If, on the other hand, you are not 100 per cent sure about whether to buy or not, or you are not sure how much you would like to offer, it is better to sleep on it. It is better to postpone an offer than to regret a purchase decision later. People have used the building inspection or financing condition clause to get out of their deals when the buyer's remorse syndrome hits, but this is not recommended.

The Seller's Motivations

When you decide on how much to offer on a property, if possible, try to find out what the seller's motivations are and structure your offer correspondingly. Many times the seller's real estate agent will be up front about his client's motivations to sell in order to encourage offers on the property. Is the seller in a hurry to sell? Has the seller bought a new home and does he need the funds of this sale to finance it? Or, is the seller being transferred to a different location by his employer and needs to move tomorrow? Other reasons a seller may want to move quickly could be illness of a family member, or any change in the family situation, such as moving in with his elderly parents, or taking over the parent's homestead, or separation or divorce from a spouse. Sometimes the seller simply makes indications of his or her eagerness to sell in the wording of the advertisement, for example: "All offers will be considered!" Is the seller's real estate agent telling you, "Make us an offer! We look at all offers!"? As a buyer, when you sense you are dealing with a seller who is in a hurry to sell, you could try to take advantage of the situation by offering less than you would otherwise have offered, and/or be tougher and more headstrong in your negotiations with the seller.

The Structure of the Offer

A typical offer includes "subject to" clauses such as "subject to financing," "subject to a home inspection," "subject to viewing the minutes of the strata corporation," etc. Moreover, it is always recommended that you make an offer "subject to seeking legal advice" and "subject to a title search," giving your lawyer the chance to review all documentation given to you by the listing real estate agent and confirm the legitimate registered owner of the property for sale. Furthermore, making the offer "subject to financing" may also be a good idea as this could give you an easy way out if you change your mind the day after signing the purchase agreement.

"Subject to financing" means that you, the buyer, will decide if you are able to arrange financing to your satisfaction.

However, as a buyer you must also consider how strong your offer will appear to the seller. Your offer could be placed ahead of another offer if it is not subject to financing and comes with pre-approved financing in place for the correct amount and correct time frame. You could also make your offer more appealing to the seller by setting a closer completion date or increasing the deposit you pay.

One of the most astute "subject to" clauses to put into a purchase agreement is "subject to an official property appraisal." Then, should the appraised value fall significantly below the agreed-upon purchase price in the contract, the potential buyer has the option to walk away from the purchase agreement.

As the buyer, you can stipulate any subject in the purchase agreement that would benefit you, even if it is a very unusual condition. An example of such an unusual "subject to" clause may be "subject to liking the drinking water on the neighbour's property," which would give you an idea of what your drinking water would be like if you drilled a well on the newly acquired acreage. When buying acreage, it is also recommended to verify borderlines and size of your new property, so you may want a clause that deals especially with surveying.

Larger real estate agencies provide their clients with a whole catalogue of "subject to" clauses on their contract forms. It is best for you, when viewing the property, to make a mental note of how to add extra protection for your interests.

Setting Your Own Limits

Whenever you put in an offer to buy a property, decide what your maximum offer will be. Nevertheless, there are qualitative differences concerning your financial flexibility. First, it depends on whether you are buying the property to live in or buying as a financial asset. If you are buying your own home, you may be inclined to offer more. If you are buying an investment, you have to adhere to your own profit calculations more strictly. Second, the market cycle will dictate aspects of your offer when the market is "at the top," but will allow greater freedom when it is near the bottom of a cycle.

Imagine you have found your dream property. In this case, you might stay just slightly below the asking price in your offer, or you could come in at full price. In the first scenario, your buyer's real estate agent will show flexibility when negotiating on your behalf. Assuming you have been looking on the market for an extended period of time to find that gem, you will not yield to the competition—unless the asking price becomes ridiculously high as it can occasionally in the case of a bidding war.

Now let us consider a situation where you have some money to invest and you see a growth opportunity in real estate. In this case, you have to buy at a competitive price because, ultimately, the profit you can make with your investment depends to a high degree on the price you pay for the property. Even if the market moves in an upward direction after you have bought the property, and it might look as if you could make a nice profit, you still have to deduct all the costs associated with the purchase and the sale of the property to estimate your potential gain.

It pays to be very selective in the amount and timing of your offer. If there is a chance that the seller might accept an offer slightly below market value, you are ahead of the game right from the beginning. On the other hand, if you pay more than market value, you need a guarantee that the real estate market will rise to new highs so that you can still make a profit. If you invest at the bottom of a real estate cycle, you will have time to get a professional appraisal of your project and structure your offer accordingly. In a booming market, make your own market analysis to balance price and risk before putting in an offer.

You lately spent much of your spare time watching the real estate market go up and up and up and you have become convinced that an investment property would be the smartest way to invest your money. You have studied the graphs of the market gurus, which show the growth of housing market values exceeding inflation figures by a decent percentage over time. And you know that your borrowing costs could be partially or fully covered by rental income. How should your approach be reflected in your offer? As an investor, you will handle your offer with discipline. You will be on the lookout for a good deal, and, when you find one, you will be well prepared and act fast. If other investors spot the same property, you will not overstep your preset limits, but will make an offer slightly below—or at—market value.

Meeting the Seller Halfway

Under normal conditions, when the real estate market is balanced—neither at a market top nor at a market bottom—you may follow certain strategies when you put in an offer. It might be a successful strategy to assume that the seller will possibly meet you halfway between his asking price and your initial offer. When you rely on this tactic, start your first offer accordingly. If, in the bidding process, your financial limit is exceeded, you are better off to stop bidding. You can always walk away and try again when the next chance presents itself.

As long as you and the seller believe that the price at the halfway point is fair, there is a reasonable expectation that you will arrive at a deal. But, there always is a chance that you may end up in negotiations with an inexperienced market participant, and it would be necessary to adjust to that particular situation. You might find Leslie's story interesting:

Leslie's Story

Leslie made a nice profit when she sold her 2003, two-bedroom investment condo. She sold the condo because she disagreed with the strata board's shoe-string budget management policies.

When she was in the market for a new investment, the first offer she made on a property met with a competing offer, so she withdrew. She made an offer on a second condo, but the owner thought it was too low and did not accept it. Then, for family reasons and because of a holiday she'd planned for a long time, Leslie's attention drifted from the real estate market.

More than three months later she again checked the market in search of a new property. She was utterly amazed that that second condo she had placed an offer on had just been sold for exactly the price she had offered, and this was three months later, and in a time when real estate board statistics showed heavy activity with upwards price movements.

Learn from this story: Market statistics show averages and give broad information about trends. With a slight variation, Leslie's offer would have had a chance of being accepted if only she had further pursued the subject. Also, time and again, houses and condos come immediately back on the market because "subject to" clauses are not met. The most common of these clauses that prevent sales from going through are "subject to financing," "subject to home inspection," and "subject to the sale of my present home." If your offer has been unsuccessful, it may be smart to follow up the situation because you just might have a second chance to buy that property.

Taking Photos of Your New Property

After your offer has been accepted, ask your real estate agent to take a few photos inside your new house, townhouse, or condominium and include all special items and accessories you have just bought (digital cameras are great for this!). For example, your purchase agreement may include window coverings, ceiling fans, chandeliers, expensive bathroom fixtures, mirrors, and appliances. These items should be listed individually in your contract of purchase. Sometimes people change their minds on how important such things are to them and they exchange a few items for less expensive ones—or you may end up with no fans or no chandeliers! It is in your best interest that nothing can be physically changed in or on the property between the date of the contract of purchase and sale and the date of completion. The photos provide documentation in case any dispute should arise. Outdoor photographs are also recommended for a nicely treed acreage to prevent the seller from realizing any timber value after selling the property to you.

The Dilemma: To Buy First or To Sell First

Should you wait until you have sold your present home and then go out and buy your new home? Or, should you first find a decent replacement for that beloved old home before you sell it? These questions are difficult to answer. Generally speaking, if you are sure you want to sell your current home, it is best to sell first and buy only once you have pocketed the funds from this sale. This way, you are under no time pressure to realize the sale, and you can wait until a buyer offers you the maximum sale price that you can reasonably hope for. However, what should you do if you just stumble upon your new dream home by chance and need the funds from the sale of your current home to finance this dream home? You have two options to deal with this situation.

Here is your first option: if you believe that your current home is easily saleable, you could visit your banker or mortgage broker and ask for bridge financing. This would allow you to put a firm offer on your dream home, with the completion date of your purchase as far out as possible, and in the meantime try to sell your current home. In essence, for a short period of time—possibly a few months—you would effectively be the owner of two homes. However, can you afford the bridge financing interest on the purchase price of your new home for the time it takes until you receive the funds from the sale of your current home? In other words, do you have a secure, well-paying job with the appropriate monthly income? Is your overall debt level low enough so that you can temporarily carry the debt of owning a second home and still sleep well at night? And, have you set a reasonable asking price for your current home to allow for a quick sale? Owning two homes at once can be very risky, as the market can turn against you the moment you buy your second home. As a worst case scenario, the real estate market could take a dip in that short period of time that you own both properties. With two homes, your losses would be multifold. Your personal banker might share his outlook on the market situation with you. Don't hesitate to ask.

Here is your second option: you put in an offer on your dream home subject to the sale of your current home. This enables you to take your chosen new home off the market while you wait to sell your current home. In a hot market, the seller may or may not entertain such an offer. If the seller does accept your conditional offer, you still risk loosing out on the purchase of your dream home in the event that a second, completely unconditional offer, is presented to the seller. In this scenario, you would have forty-eight hours to remove all your conditions including the condition "subject to the sale of my current home," or else walk away from the offer altogether. Nevertheless, if another purchaser is not able to write an offer with no conditions, your purchase contract is protected until you remove all your subjects.

Conclusion

Before you make an offer on any property, think it over carefully. Consider the following:

- Is this really your dream home?
- Does the property represent good value?
- Is this the best investment property you can possibly find?
- Will this investment have a guaranteed positive cash-flow and/or have lots of potential upward appreciation?

Only if you answer these questions affirmatively should you consider the next step and make an offer. Then, act quickly so that another buyer does not snap the property away right in front of your eyes. When the market is near the top, this could be just a matter of hours. When preparing an offer, carefully consider the "subject to" clauses you would like to include in your offer. If you change your mind, "subject to" clauses could ultimately be your only way out of a binding legal agreement.

When deciding on how much to offer, your speedy and up-to-date research on the property, together with comparative recent sales in the area, can help with your decision making process. Adjust your offer strategies to the situation and keep your real estate agent well informed so he or she can be most efficient in negotiations on your behalf. Play out in your mind how the seller may react to your offer and accept or counter it. Plan out your next step in advance. Throughout the negotiation process, stay disciplined and keep in mind your spending limit. Remember, you want to adhere to your budget and your financial limits. And also keep in mind how sincerely you really want this property. If it is an investment property, certainly you don't want to overstep your limits. If it is your dream home that you will enjoy for many years to come, your rationalization may be different.

Key Points

- How much should you offer?
  - ❖ Ask your real estate agent for a market analysis on how much comparative properties sold for.
  - ❖ Take into account deficiencies.
  - ❖ Consider the seller's motivations.
  - ❖ Decide how desperately you want it.
  - ❖ Ask if offers are accepted on brand-new housing.
- Strategies: do you want to present …
  - ❖ … a fair offer?
  - ❖ … an offer below asking price?
  - ❖ … an offer at full price?
  - ❖ … a competing offer above full price?
  - ❖ … an offer below or at market value?
  - ❖ … an offer to eventually meet the seller half way?
- Structure of the offer:
  - ❖ Include all necessary "subject to" conditions.
  - ❖ Decide how long to leave the offer open.
- Preset a maximum limit on how much to offer.
- Other potential buyers' "subject to" clauses may not be met and the home may be back on the market for you to try for again with a slightly modified offer.
- When your offer is accepted, take documentation photos of the interior, exterior and grounds.
- Your own home: sell first and then buy the new home, or, find replacement first and then sell your old home.

PART THREE:

THE PROCESS OF RENTING AND SELLING PROPERTY

Chapter 12:

Renting Out Your Property

You may not wish to sell your "old" property when you move on; you may prefer to rent it out. Or, you may have acquired a property with the idea to use it for rental income. Now you have two options: you can do all the work yourself, or you can enter into a contract with a property management firm to do the work for you. There is also the question of how to prepare for and deal with vacancies, which sometimes seem to be unavoidable. And, finally, as a landlord you can be a step ahead if you know your way around some important tax issues that pertain to your rental properties.

Working with a Property Management Firm

There are very good reasons to have a professional manager do the work for you. It may be that you live in another city or town or that you don't always have the time to take care of everything necessary. If you hire a good, professional property management firm, you can be assured that your rental unit will be well maintained. Property management firms take care of leaky roofs, blown-away skylights, water damage, exploding hot water tanks, etc. The firm will have an on-call service twenty-four hours a day, seven days a week that will take this load off your shoulders. The larger firms have crews who do the repairs themselves; the smaller firms contract out the repair work to subcontractors. Here the question, of course, arises: Are these subcontractors fair and reliable?

A property management firm will enter a contract with you—usually for a year—with distinct clauses for termination. There is a fee structure for these services; industry standard is approximately 10 per cent of your rental income. If you own more than one rental unit, you may be able to negotiate a lower rate.

When a property management firm does all the advertising for your rental unit to find a tenant, and later has the rental contract signed on your behalf, your identity as owner is not revealed. Instead, there is a professional relationship exclusively between the property manager and the tenant. This leads to another advantage for you. Professional management will enable you to avoid any kind of personal conflict with an unsuitable applicant or tenant, which is especially good in case of an eviction.

Another service you receive from the property management firm is a monthly profit and loss statement and a balance sheet of your account. On the income statement, the property management fees are deducted from the rental income, together with costs of any repairs, maintenance, strata fees, advertising expenses and, possibly, insurance premiums, mortgage payments, and property taxes, depending on your business arrangement with your management firm. Whatever is left in funds is transferred to your personal bank account. On the balance sheet, assets (tenant security deposits and cash in the bank) are offset by the liabilities (accounts payable, and capital—retained earnings and owner's draw). So, all the accounting is done for you.

A good property management firm also takes care that your rental unit does not remain vacant after a tenant gives notice. They advertise your rental unit and work hard to have continuous lease contracts so you will enjoy a continued flow of income. Property managers do block advertising in newspapers and on the Internet; some tenants looking for new accommodation prefer such well-managed units instead of having to deal with various types of landlords, who might be more or less efficient.

Also, when you work with a property management firm, there is no need to be afraid of possibly losing several months rent in the case of a non-paying tenant you would like to have evicted. Teaming up with a property manager spares you having to go through the dispute resolution process if you are not comfortable with this kind of situation. The monthly management fee for the property manager more than balances your possible loss. The property manager represents you in court. Paying a fee to a property manager frees you from any disagreeable involvement with a difficult tenant when there are unforeseen problems, such as an eviction. A property manager is licensed and has the know-how. He or she knows the Residential Tenancy Act and applies rules and regulations to the letter. (The rules and regulations for eviction differ from province to province.)

Before a rental agreement is signed, the manager carefully screens the prospective tenants and undertakes credit and reference checks. Problems may show up, but your manager has the means to ensure that they will not linger on. Your manager collects the rent on the first of every month, and includes late payment fees when they apply. Make sure your contract with your manager stipulates an inspection schedule so you will not be surprised if a tenant subleases rooms to his buddies, or the lady who signed a no-pet agreement is keeping a schnauzer on the property. Again, should any dispute arise from these or other issues, your property manager will represent you through the dispute resolution process or at court. (This again differs from province to province.)

When you search for a good property manager, word of mouth can do wonders. You will also find a listing of local property management firms in the Yellow Pages and on the Internet. Some good advice is to call the firm of your choice and see how long it takes for them to call you back. You can ask how long the firm has been in business and how many licensed property managers they employ. You can also study the block advertisements of a property management firm to find out about the effort and creativity the firm puts into advertising their suites, condos, townhouses, or houses for rent.

Renting the Property out Yourself

You may indeed want to be in charge of renting out your property yourself. This may be the case if you own a basement suite in your house or if you have just bought a duplex. First of all, you need to familiarize yourself with the Residential Tenancy Act. It is available in the reference section of your local library as well as on the Internet. These laws differ from province to province. Once you have screened all applicants and chosen who will move into your rental unit, you must fill in the standard residential tenancy agreement so that it holds up in court, if it ever comes to that. You must know your tenants' rights when it comes to you giving them notice on the one side and you must know your rights if, for example, you wish to vacate your rental unit so that you can take in your elderly parents. When it becomes convenient for you to use your rental unit for your relatives, the tenant enjoys special rights. Also, when you have the intention to move and sell your property, tenants' rights are protected. For example, in British Columbia you must give your tenant two months' written notice and reimburse the tenant one month's rent, meaning he or she will have the last month of occupancy free. So it is important to choose the right tenant, and it is important for both parties to abide by the law. Novice landlords are probably best advised to refrain from trying to interpret the Residential Tenancy Act themselves; they should seek professional advice.

Credit Checks

A credit check is a standard procedure—and for good reason. You don't know the person who wants to move into your rental suite that might be worth $250,000 to $300,000. On the phone you only hear the friendly voice: "Is it still available?"

And when you interview the applicant in person, you are not allowed to ask the questions that might interest you the most: How is your income situation? How is your credit rating? Have you ever declared bankruptcy? Here, it is a good custom to follow established routines. After you have interviewed a person who has made a good impression on you, and before you sign a lease agreement, you perform a credit check and you check the applicant's references. The objectivity of a credit check will give you peace of mind. And last, remember that, by law, you need to get a prospective tenant's written permission to do a credit check. For a credit check, you'll need the applicant's full name, Social Insurance Number (SIN), birth date, and present address.

One way of doing a credit check as a private person is to become a member of a local rental property owners' association. Other resources may also be available through this association, such as a list of evicted tenants and/or a list of tenants in the area who are behind on their rent payments. A rental owners' association offers a great variety of services to landlords: legal advice by phone, credit checks on prospective tenants, educational seminars, advertising, and insurance, as well as discounts when working with recommended contractors. The association can also provide you with all of the legal forms necessary, such as application for tenancy forms and a standard residential tenancy agreement that protects your rights as a landlord while fostering worry-free landlord/tenant relations.

Discrimination in Residential Tenancy

When seeking a new tenant for your rental unit, it is imperative that you are familiar with Section 10 of the Human Rights Code. This section prohibits discrimination in tenancies based on a person's race, colour, place of origin, religion, marital status, family status, physical or mental disability, gender, sexual orientation, age, or lawful source of income. For example, you cannot turn down an applicant for the sole reason that the applicant has children. Equally, as income assistance is considered a lawful source of income, you cannot refuse to rent to someone just on the basis that he or she is receiving income assistance. The Human Rights Tribunal deals with all cases of discrimination.

Step-by-step Instructions on How to Rent Out Your Rental Suite Yourself

Step 1: Analyze the rental market in the area of your rental property to get a comparative overview and to establish the correct rent price. The local paper or the Internet can give you all the information you need.

Step 2: Advertise. This can be done in the local newspaper, where you can chose between advertising a day or two, all week, or only on weekends, depending on your budget and the response you get. Weekend advertising is usually more expensive, but can be especially effective as more people have time to read the newspaper on the weekend and to go to showings of properties for rent.

Rental sites on the Internet are also an effective advertising medium. They are less expensive than newspaper advertising, or even free. The cost of advertising on the Internet is per ad, not per word, as is the case with newspaper advertising. Internet advertising offers the advantage of describing your property in full length and in detail, outlining its best features so you can attract only those who are genuinely interested. You can also post photos on these rental sites on the Internet.

The way you formulate and highlight features of your rental suite, together with the price, will make a difference in who will apply. Think of what benefits your property offers to the prospective tenant and mention these benefits in your ad. For example, you could say things like: nice view, extra-large balcony, walk to shops and theatre, close to the community center, or, nice backyard. Also, if your ad states that you will require credit checks and references, prospective tenants will get the impression that your unit is well managed. Some people are looking for these features, while others will be deterred by them.

An additional way to find a good tenant and avoiding some of the cost of advertising is simply to look at the "accommodation wanted" section of your local newspaper. This is where people put up there own ads and tell you what they are looking for and sometimes add what specifically qualifies them as good tenants.

Finally you can advertise your house for rent with your own "for rent" sign on the lawn.

Step 3: Take down the name and the phone number of everyone who calls. Also, it is a good idea to take notes of the telephone conversation for future reference. If you are advertising on the Internet, you can choose to reply only to those inquiries that seem sincere, polite, and promising.

Step 4: Show your rental suite with the least amount of delay possible. Good tenants most likely will view several properties and you don't want to lose a good applicant only because you made him or her wait several days before showing your property.

Also, avoid becoming too friendly with an applicant while showing your rental property. At this time, you have no idea what the applicant's qualifications are, and if you would ever consider him or her as your future tenant.

Step 5: Have the applicant(s) fill out a standard application form. This should include the applicant's and co-applicant's full legal names, dates of birth, SINs, present and previous addresses, and landlord information, present and past employer information, banking information including credit card numbers, personal references, etc. Other adult occupants, minor occupants, and any pets should also be disclosed.

Make sure that all applicants sign and date their application forms, thereby enabling you to verify all the information given; you are now legally entitled to perform employer, landlord, reference, and credit checks. Last, do not sign the application for tenancy form yourself unless you have already made up your mind to accept an applicant as your new tenant.

It can be very helpful in your decision making process to watch as applicants fill out their applications, rather than allowing the applicants to take the applications home to fill out. You will notice the amount of effort the applicants put into filling out their forms correctly. For example, if an applicant phones his or her family or workplace in order to get information needed to fill out the application correctly, you can assume you are most likely dealing with an honest person.

Step 6: Check all the information given on the application form to make sure that it is correct.

Step 7: Check all references provided by the applicant and perform a credit check.

Step 8: If you think you have found a suitable applicant, let him or her sign the rental agreement and don't waste time with more showings or interviews. You don't want to lose a good applicant just because you delayed your decision for too long.

Step 9: Fill out a standard residential tenancy agreement, have the tenant sign it, and sign it yourself.

Step 10: Insist on a security deposit equal to half the monthly rent, in addition to a pet deposit, if applicable.

Step 11: Do a walk-through with the tenant and fill out a conditions inspection report. Record the condition of the suite prior to the move-in and prior to handing over the keys to your new tenant. A signed conditions inspection report helps resolve any disagreements at the time the tenant moves out, when you do a final check against this document.

Step 12: Perform a sixty-day inspection to ensure that the new tenant is taking good care of your property. For any kind of inspection, you have to give proper notice.

Step 13: Perform annual routine inspections of your rental suite to ensure everything is in good order.

Situations that Put You in a Position to End a Tenancy Legally

As stipulated in the Residential Tenancy Act of British Columbia, as a landlord you can end a tenancy only if you have valid reasons to do so. Examples of valid reasons are unpaid rent, unpaid utilities, and unreasonable conduct by the tenant—or your desire to occupy the premises yourself or use it for your close family. To end a tenancy, you must fill out the appropriate Notice to End Tenancy form and hand it over to your tenant. Keep a copy of this form, as it may be required during a later dispute resolution.

Each province has its own regulations about how a landlord can end a tenancy. Check with the appropriate government branch.

Vacancies

A vacancy can become a terrible headache. Whenever you depend on others to help you pay your mortgage or your credit lines, you have to count on surprises. Over time, not everything will run smoothly, so you have to budget for the unforeseen minor shortfalls that are inevitable. You must have a rainy-day fund. If you decide that selling would be the best way out of an unpleasant situation, you must keep in mind that generally a house or a condo is not sold in a day. Emergency funds have to be available if you aim to be a smart investor.

Further, there are all kinds of reasons why people might want to get out of a rental agreement. For example, in the middle of winter, just when it is the most difficult to find replacements for tenants, your tenants may lose their jobs, fall ill, move in as caretakers with elderly parents, get married, or inherit some money.

Vacancies are a possibility. Finding new tenants also involves extra costs for advertising, cleaning, and so on.

Pets

Do you allow pets? Allowing pets generally means additional wear on your suite; this is why the law allows you to take a pet deposit. However, if you have difficulty finding a tenant for your suite, which you have advertised as "no pets allowed," you do have the option to broaden the number of potential good applicants by changing your pet policy to "a pet will be considered." This could be a successful step if you cannot afford financially to have your suite sit empty any longer. These days, some very nice people are living by themselves and love to have pets as their company—and these people make very good tenants.

Rental Property and Taxes

It is to your advantage to know some of the tax applications regarding your rental property.

- *Claim your GST rebate.* If you buy a brand-new house, townhouse, or condominium, you will have to add GST to your purchase price, unless it is already included. If you did not buy the property for your own use, but rather to lease it out to a tenant, the Canada Revenue Agency (CRA) allows you to have the GST rebate refunded back to you. However, you need to show to the CRA that the property is intended as a true rental property, not to be flipped soon after the purchase. This requirement is generally addressed by presenting a lease agreement of a minimum of one year's duration. When you want to claim back your GST rebate portion, all you need to do is to go to the CRA Web site and download the GST New Rental Housing Rebate form. Once you have completed this form (of course, your accountant may also complete it for you), attach it to a copy of your minimum one-year rental lease as well as a copy of your purchaser's statement of adjustments. You can then drop the entire package off at the Canada Revenue Agency in person or mail it by Express Post; the sooner you hand in your application, the sooner you will receive the government refund check in the mail, which you can then apply against your credit line or mortgage payments.

- *Do not claim depreciation on your property in a rising market.* According to tax laws, claiming yearly depreciation is optional. This means that, when filing your personal income tax, you will have a choice of calculating a yearly amount of depreciation for the wear and tear on your property. Historically, in an environment where the real estate market values were stable and not rising, it made good sense to calculate a depreciation figure and write down the net book value of your property as the property aged year after year. Today, whether you decide to claim depreciation or not should be influenced by the current state of the market cycle and the amount of time you intend to hold on to the property. For an extended period of time now, land values have risen a lot faster than buildings have depreciated, leaving you with a net gain. These days, when you put your house or condo up for sale after holding on to it for several years, the structure will have aged, yet you will still be able to earn a nice profit because prices are rising so much. If, in this kind of environment, you previously filed your income taxes making use of the option of depreciation, you will pay higher capital gains tax when you sell your rental property because the depreciation diminished the net book value of your property. If, in your judgment, prices will continue to rise, it is to your advantage to not calculate any yearly depreciation on your property when you file your taxes. Thus, at the time of the sale of your property, the figure shown as your taxable profit—the difference between the sale price and the net book value—will be smaller and you will save on capital gains tax. Nevertheless, be aware of your choice because you may not know how long you will keep your property as the market is cyclical.

- *Deduct any mortgage interest from your rental income.* This can save you a lot of money. If your personal situation is such that you own a principal residence and also invest in a rental property, and you have considerable equity built up, it is advisable that you load all the necessary credit on your rental property. This will allow you to deduct all your financing expenses from you rental income, reducing the overall tax payment. The rule is that, if a mortgage or credit line is used to produce a stream of income, mortgage or credit line interest is tax deductible.

- *Consider the pros and cons of RRSP contributions versus paying off your debt.* Should you pay down your mortgage or put that money into your Registered Retirement Savings Plan (RRSP)? You will ask yourself this question at least once a year before the RRSP deadline on February 28. There might be advantages on both sides of the equation, and much depends on your circumstances.

As a first step, consider your current age. If you have only a few years left before you retire, paying off your mortgage is possibly the better option for you. With less income to expect down the road, you will wish to be free of mortgage payments. Furthermore, your tax rate will also decrease proportionally as your income decreases.

However, if you are still in your prime working years and possibly in a high-income tax bracket, putting money into an RRSP may be more beneficial, as this money can accumulate and multiply for many years to come without you needing to pay any tax on the income or capital appreciation. Moreover, unless you are going to collect a hefty pension, in your retirement years you will most likely be in a lower income tax bracket than you are currently, so when you do finally take the money out of your RRSP, it will be taxed at a lower rate.

Money you put into your RRSP today will lower your tax payments right now, which is always nice. Your accountant can tell you how much money you save on your taxes for every dollar you put into your RRSP. He can also tell you, by looking at your current personal income tax situation, how much money you should put into your RRSP for the current year to offset other income. This "saved money" you can then spend on other things; for example, you could pay down your credit line or make a lump sum payment on your mortgage.

If you decide to put money into your RRSP rather than paying off your mortgage or your credit line, you'll have more debt outstanding and, therefore, higher interest payments; on your tax return these interest payments can be deducted from rental income, thereby giving you the advantage of paying less tax on your rental property.

- *Application of capital gains tax versus regular income tax is a consideration when timing the sale of your rental property.* To be eligible for capital gains taxation, you have to fulfill certain criteria. The timing of your sale will have important tax implications. If the choice is all yours and time is on your side, it is rather beneficial for your pocketbook to know the details of these taxation rules. It is important to realize that the Canada Revenue Agency draws a fine line between what is considered income and what is considered capital gain.

If you have held your rental property for several years, there is no question that it is a true rental property and, therefore, any profit you make on the sale will be considered a capital gain. As such, only 50 per cent of the profit will be taxable.

However, if you frequently buy and sell properties and do not hold them for an extended period of time, this may be considered as flipping. The Canada Revenue Agency could argue that you are in the business of buying and selling real estate and your profit upon selling your properties is therefore considered income and not a capital gain. In this case, your sales profit would be 100 per cent taxable.

If you are making it your business to flip properties, you could also talk to your accountant about possibly incorporating this business, so that consequently you'll be taxed at a lower business tax rate.

Conclusion

Sometimes tenants may become your best friends. It might be a relationship of mutual respect or total neutrality. And then there are cases where a tenancy ends in outright hostilities. Be aware of these possibilities, especially if the place you want to rent out is your former home and you, of course, are sentimentally attached to it. Another issue is living in close proximity to your tenants when your house is large enough and you want mortgage helpers, or you own a duplex. These are situations where it is most unlikely that you would want professional management.

Before you make renting out property part of your daily life, ask yourself the following questions: Am I good at property management? Do I enjoy property management? Do I have the time to do it efficiently? Do I think I could collect the monthly rent with no problems? Am I comfortable representing myself in court if I become involved in a disagreement? Do I have a family member or partner who could help manage my rental unit? What is my past experience with managing a rental unit?

On the other hand, if the decision to manage your rental unit yourself or have it done professionally is more or less a business decision, remember that a property manager will ask roughly 10 per cent of your rental income for his firm's professional services. But such an expense could be more than offset by the profit you could make when selling your older units into a market that goes up and up, and then acquiring new units when the market has calmed down. You may also be busy with another full-time professional career and don't have the time, patience, or energy to look after your rental properties yourself.

To make an informed decision about which opportunities are worth pursuing, you should have a basic knowledge about taxes, and you should work with an experienced and knowledgeable accountant who can help you to identify critical issues like timing of your sale, or, when working with borrowed money, putting mortgages on your rental units, so you can deduct interest payments as expenses, etc.

Key Points

- Why work with a property management firm?
  - ❖ You don't have the expertise.
  - ❖ You don't have the time.
  - ❖ You don't want to disclose your identity.
  - ❖ Your properties are out of town.

- Services of a property management firm:
  - ❖ Finding a suitable tenant
  - ❖ Collecting the rent
  - ❖ Emergency and standard repair services
  - ❖ Accounting
  - ❖ Routine inspections of the property
  - ❖ Professional advice
  - ❖ Representation in court

- Advantages of renting out property yourself:
  - ❖ Save on property management fees
  - ❖ Take active part in the decision making process; for example, selection of tenant, etc.

- What you should know when renting out property yourself:
  - ❖ Familiarize yourself with the rules and regulations.
  - ❖ Possibly become a member of a rental owners' association.
  - ❖ Beware of discrimination. Use standard application forms.
  - ❖ Perform credit checks and reference checks.
  - ❖ Use standard residential tenancy agreement.
  - ❖ Fill out a condition inspection report prior to move-in.
  - ❖ Perform routine inspections.

- Taxes
  - ❖ On new housing, claim back the GST rebate if it is a true rental property.
  - ❖ In a rising housing market, you may not want to calculate any depreciation.
  - ❖ Deduct interest expenses from your rental income.
  - ❖ Evaluate the pros and cons of paying down your mortgage versus making RRSP investments.
  - ❖ When flipping properties, profit could be taxed as income instead of capital gains taxation applicable for rental property held over an extended period of time.

Chapter 13:

You want to Sell your Property

Everybody wants to sell for the highest price possible. A variety of factors blend together to enable you to realize maximum market value and realize your highest profit. Working with a good listing real estate agent is paramount in achieving the most successful sale possible of your property.

Documentation

When you meet with your listing real estate agent, he or she will ask you for the following documentation:

- Your purchase contract or property tax notice showing the legal description of the property.
- Your property tax notice showing the assessed value of the property.
- The original disclosure statement of the property, if you bought brand-new.
- A site survey with the measurements of the lot and house or condo or townhouse unit, and any floor plans you may have.
- For property on a strata, the rules and regulations, the minutes of the last twenty-four months, and the financial statements.

The Listing Real Estate Agent

Finding a Good Listing Real Estate Agent

When you are looking for a real estate agent to sell your property, the real estate agent that previously served you well might come to your mind. Also, word of mouth travels fast and, when you tell your friends that you are in the market to sell your property, they will pass on their experiences. Do they know a good agent with great negotiation skills? If you are new to the area or a first-timer and you want to get a feeling for the personality of some local real estate agents, you could attend open houses and informally establish contact until you find a real estate agent you like. Or, if you yourself are in the process of doing a comparative market analysis to establish the worth of your house before putting it on the market, you probably will arrange to view similar properties in your neighbourhood. The listing real estate agents of these properties could assist you with their services. You can study these professionals in action; the more an agent impresses you, the better. To find a good agent, you could also turn to the real estate section of the local newspaper where the large real estate agencies feature the names and photos of the real estate agents who have been named for awards over the past year. Another place to look is in large shopping malls where real estate agents often maintain showroom space for their listings, and real estate agents of the big agencies take turns running these showrooms.

You need to know what kind of person you would like to work with. Are you looking for a great negotiator who can get you the price you want? Or somebody with heaps of creativity when it comes to advertising and staging your property? Are you looking for a competent agent with many years of experience? Or, are you looking for a problem-solving agent who can think quickly and will go the extra mile to come up with all the right answers to whatever questions or concerns that arise when selling your property? This may be all the more necessary if you are from out of town, or you are a very busy professional, or you are a senior, or you are in a hurry to sell. Probably the most important trait of an excellent listing real estate agent is that he or she is able to do a correct and precise market evaluation and, therefore, suggest the most accurate and best selling price for your property.

The Discount Listing Real Estate Agent

If you don't have a favourite full-commission real estate agent, and you want to save on commission because you believe that, when you don't need to pay as high a commission, your sales price can be a little bit lower and thus be more competitive in the market, you could consider working with a discount real estate agent. There is certainly a niche for such thinking. That is where the "one fee" real estate agents or the real estate agents who work for 1 per cent of the sales price find their place. The main feature of this category of real estate agents is that their fee structure is different, and you pay less commission for their services. With a full-service and full-commission real estate agent, the commission that the seller needs to pay is usually calculated on the final sales figure. The commission rate for the services of a full-commission real estate agent ranges from 6 per cent on the first $100,000 and 3 per cent on the balance, to 7 per cent on the first $100,000 and 4 per cent on the balance. Keep in mind that you can usually negotiate with your full-commission agent whether you wish to pay the higher fee structure in order to make it more attractive for other real estate agents to bring their clients, or whether you prefer the lower fee structure in order to save on commission payment. In either case, with full-commission service, the higher the final sales price, the more commission you pay to your agent.

With a flat-fee discount service, you pay a flat fee. In the case of the One Percent Realty Ltd. firms operating in Alberta and British Columbia, depending on the sales price of your home, you pay either the minimum commission of $5,800, including disbursements, for the sale of any home listed at $500,000 or less, or 1 per cent of the sales price plus $800 in disbursements for the sale of a home listed above $500,000. In essence, the higher the price of the property sold, the greater the savings when using this discount service in comparison to using a full-commission firm.

On the other hand, a discount real estate agent may provide full service or only partial service. This is usually based on the fee you are willing to pay. For example, with One Percent Realty, one difference in service in comparison to the full-commission agencies is the mode of communication—One Percent Realty does not have a pager system through the office, but rather the real estate agent personally answers calls. An example of partial service, which may be available for as little as $500 in commissions by other specific discount real estate agencies, would be only a listing of the property on the MLS with no other obligations—no showings by the real estate agent, no open houses, etc.

Probably the biggest disadvantage when working with a discount broker is that other real estate agents looking for properties for their buyers may be hesitant to show their clients your property, as they know their commission for their sale effort will be less than what they would get if they facilitated a purchase of a property listed for sale by a full-commission realty firm. Therefore, your property may get fewer showings and, hence, the chance of an offer or even multiple offers on your property is also lower. Working with a discount commission broker is certainly not advisable when you already know that you will be in a hurry to sell. On the other hand, there are plenty of buyers out there who search for themselves on the Internet or in the local real estate paper. These potential buyers will check out your property if it suits their purpose and price, and they then could contact your discount commissions real estate agent for a viewing.

Here is an example of a real estate deal where the seller saved himself a considerable amount of money on the commissions he needed to pay to his real estate agent:

Tom's Story

Tom put his investment property up for sale, using the services of a discount real estate agency. With his discount real estate agent, he had agreed on a flat fee of $5,600 in commission and fees, regardless of the final sale price. Once his place was well advertised he then received two offers. The first offer came in well below Tom's expected price, thus he did not accept it. A few weeks passed before a second offer came in, nearly identical to the first one. Yet, this time it was a different deal. With some encouragement from his agent, he did accept this second offer. In this case, the buyer, a family from out of province, worked with Tom's discount listing real estate agent as their buyer's real estate agent. As Tom's real estate agent represented both parties—the buyer and the seller—Tom's real estate agent offered to forego a thousand dollars of Tom's commission, as he collected two commissions for representing the seller and the buyer and was therefore financially well ahead. Tom was very happy with this discount agency. Indeed, Tom, in the end, had received more money for his investment property, as he had saved himself a few thousand dollars on the commission for working with a discount agent and another thousand dollars because his agent offered him an additional discount when he collected two commissions for representing both the buyer and the seller.

Learn from this story: Your choice of real estate agent depends on your needs. Full-scale real estate agencies and discount real estate agencies both do an excellent job, but you have to decide which type of service will better suit your needs. If the listing real estate agent also represents the buyer, her or she may step into the negotiation process and forego some of the commission in order for the deal to go through and therefore allow the agent to collect two commissions.

Showing Your Home

Sell "As Is" or Renovate?

When people put their houses up for sale, the same questions always arise—how to attract buyers, how to sell faster, and how to get a better price are just the most obvious. But, besides your asking price, curb appeal and first impressions are most significant. They may be the most important aspects in attracting potential buyers because most people will make up their minds after that first look at your property as they drive by. So you, the seller, should put yourself in the shoes of those potential buyers. If the outside is attractive, potential buyers will be tempted to get a look inside, and this is the first step to a fast sale. To achieve this goal, mow the lawn, trim the bushes and trees, and, specific to the season, plant ornamental shrubs or flowers to draw attention. If tools and toys and bikes and hoses are strewn around, driveways are cracked by tree roots or moss, and weeds are overpowering your grass, people will expect to find the same conditions of untidiness inside and will drive on.

As first impressions about the outside of your home are important, first impressions about the inside of the home are crucial as well—especially the entrance. Foremost, the place should be tidy, clean, and uncluttered. In addition, remove personal items such as photos and knickknacks so that potential buyers can picture their own belongings in their new home. Put excessive quantities of books, folders and paperwork in boxes and store them away. Put away dishes and dish towels, and hang pretty, clean towels in bathrooms.

Where wear and tear is quite obvious, some minor repairs or replacements might considerably improve the overall impression. Increasing the market value of your home with renovations may work for or against you. As with any renovation, unless you are a handyman and have the time and expertise to make updates inexpensively and efficiently, their benefits must be weighed against their cost.

Real estate agents have studied the market. To make your property more attractive for buyers, real estate agents will tell you there is a more successful strategy than trying to patch up too many things at the same time. Experience tells them that not every home improvement will raise the value of your home, so they suggest focusing on kitchens and bathrooms. Modernizing and beautifying these rooms carefully will be more cost effective and result in a better resale value and a faster sale.

There are people who can bring new life into older homes and who are able to create an amazing atmosphere. Older homes can be beautifully renovated and then successfully sold, especially homes in prime locations. But don't think it can be done on a shoestring budget. You have to have proper plans and detailed estimates. Furthermore, you absolutely need funds for cost overruns. As an example, you think a bay window would look wonderful in that sunken living room. You take out the old, small window only to discover carpenter ants and water damage. This means the reconstruction will be more expensive than originally planned.

Different people have different tastes and expectations. This is particularly true when it comes to colours, or when one potential buyer prefers wall-to-wall carpeting while another is keen on tile or hardwood floors. When it comes to this kind of renovation, some buyers might like to follow their own ideas and preferences and get a better deal on the price of the property than buy a fully updated home. But, generally speaking, it is a very good idea to put the house in move-in condition to attract a buyer. A new coat of paint can make the interior of a home look more attractive and smell like new.

Nevertheless, there are definitely things one should *not* do. Avoid painting bright colours, which may appeal to only a limited number of potential buyers. For example, avoid painting your kitchen bright blue or your bathroom deep red. Rather, go with neutral colours that appeal to the broadest sector of potential buyers. Decorating your front lawn with pink flamingos instead of flowers would fall into that same category.

Furniture and Furnishings

It is generally a good idea to show your place furnished. A furnished house gives more of a home-like impression and can be better envisioned as such by buyers than an empty house. If you have a budget for house staging, you could even consider replacing your furniture with new furniture and new accessories to make the home more attractive to potential buyers. Should your home be cluttered, you may consider taking out some furniture in order to create some open space, so that the potential buyers can get a better idea of how big the place really is.

Each room should have its own theme. For example, a room that could be the second bedroom should be clearly furnished as such, or as a guest bedroom, a child's bedroom, a child's play room, a home office, or an exercise room. Buyers should have no problem figuring out what they are looking at and ultimately what they are paying for.

Your house should be as bright a possible. Open all the blinds, pull back all the curtains, and turn on all the lights. If necessary, buy some extra table and floor lamps, both as accessories that look nice and as fixtures to make the home even brighter for evening or rainy-day showings.

Some listing real estate agents are experts in staging a home for sale. They may simply have a natural flair for this, or they have taken special courses for which they have received a "staging home certificate" from a professional college or seminar.

The Feature Sheet

A professional-looking feature sheet about your property left on the kitchen counter should welcome prospective buyers. A good feature sheet shows colour photos of the outside of your house or building, both the back and the front, accompanied by a short description of what your property has to offer. The next pages of your feature sheet should be full of colour photos of the inside of the house. Photograph all the main rooms from the best possible angles to make the rooms as attractive and spacious looking as possible. If you have a floor area analysis of all the rooms, attach it as part of the feature sheet. A map of the neighborhood and surrounding area, with your property highlighted, will further orient potential buyers. Last, the feature sheet gives all your real estate agent's contact information.

The Asking Price

As a first step, set the asking price slightly above your price expectation in order to leave room for negotiation. Most buyers like to negotiate. As this is part of human nature, prepare yourself for this exciting deal-making process. Have a preset framework of what would be acceptable for you once you have tested the market.

Your real estate agent will suggest a price range for your property. In order to form your own opinion and have a fair discussion about this most important issue, compare your property to similar properties that have recently sold in the neighbourhood. Also, your real estate agent can give you a printout of asking prices of similar houses, townhouses, or condominiums in your area, and can also provide you data on pending properties—properties with accepted offers on them but which have not closed yet. From this information you get a clear picture in how far people's expectations are met. This information can also be interpreted in terms of a buyer's or a seller's market by your agent, thus helping you in your decision making.

To calculate an average price, add up all the prices in your list and then divide by the number of properties on the list. You can then decide if you want to list for more, the same, or less than the average price.

In this process, it is important to not only compare the size, location, and the age of a property, but also the condition of the property compared to your own. You need to take into consideration the future expenses a buyer will have on your property for any repairs or necessary improvements. Does your property need new paint, new flooring, a new roof, or a new deck? Does it need a new lawn?

When performing a comparative market analysis to establish a realistic asking price, also take into consideration the value of any special upgrades you have made to your home. For example, a kitchen with tile flooring, granite countertops, and a side-by-side, ice-making fridge is worth considerably more than one with laminate flooring, Formica countertops, and a standard fridge. Or, consider the value of the large deck add-on that you had custom built. Also, add the cost of the beautiful special-ordered slate in your bathroom and slate trim around your fireplace, or the extra expense for that fabulous custom-made backsplash in your kitchen. And, don't forget the cost of the gorgeous, custom-made drapery on the windows throughout your home, which you personally chose with great finesse.

If it is your condo you want to put on the market, there are established price categories you should know about. When performing a comparative analysis on a condo, you should consider, for example:

- $6,000–$12,000 extra for underground parking
- $5,000–$10,000 extra per floor (the higher the floor, the higher the price) with the exception of a ground-floor patio unit, which may be worth as much or more than the second floor
- $10,000 extra for a private patio
- $5,000 extra for an extra large balcony
- $5,000–$10,000 extra for a corner unit
- $10,000–$15,000 or more for a nice view

Say you are too busy and you don't have time for extensive comparative market research. There is another way to find out how much your asking price should be. Invite some of your local real estate agents and ask them for their input, and then draw your conclusions based on their estimates. Work with agents who are familiar with the neighbourhood and who therefore have a good knowledge of the current local listings and their prices. These professionals will be very efficient in setting a fair price because they will know that, in providing you with a good estimate, they are also competing to get your business.

The Importance of a Realistic Asking Price

It is important to set a realistic asking price right from the beginning. Interest in a new listing generally reaches a peak in the first two to three weeks. After your property has been on the market for several weeks, the number of potential buyers will decline. Should you start off with an asking price that is too high for the market, your property may end up sitting on the market for too long and become stale-dated. Even if, at a later point, you decide to lower the asking price, there will be a chance that those potential buyers who are still in the market had noticed your property as priced too high. They may not be inclined to give it a second look, but will move on in their search. If, eventually, you do get an offer from new buyers, the offer will likely be lower than the offer you would have received when the property was first listed on the market.

In the condo market, the situation might be slightly different. Here it is much easier to establish a price range for selling a condo because of their overall similarities. But it is in this category of real estate that quite a few speculators are hoping to make money with overpriced units; these overpriced condos, however, often end up sitting on the market for a long time.

Your agent will hold an open house exclusive to other real estate agents, usually shortly after listing your property. At the open house, the pricing of your house will be discussed among the real estate agents, and their reactions will also give you an idea if your house is priced according to market.

Should your property sit on the market for several months, your real estate agent may suggest that you lower the asking price, usually by a minimum of $3,000–$5,000, or more as time goes by. Some agents prefer price reductions of $10,000 or more at a time so that the price reduction really gets noticed by potential buyers. As a rule, small and frequent price drops are not as efficient in the market place as one large drop. The decision about when and how much to drop the price will be completely yours.

However, there are always exceptions to the general rule. If you are a lucky person and you have just inherited a large tract of land with a magnificent view of the mountains or the ocean, you should set your asking price as high as you can. It might take a long time for the right person to come by, yet, for you, there is no need to lower the price because that land of yours is unique. For everybody else, the bottom line is that, when selling real estate, the market—not the seller—sets the price. However, in a scenario where you have significantly overpriced your property and you do find buyers interested and willing to pay your price, the deal may still not go through. If the buyer requires bank financing, the bank will want to appraise the property. If the appraised value falls well below the purchase price, the bank will deny the financing unless the buyer is willing to make a greater down payment.

Working with a Professional Property Appraiser

When you sell your property, you could decide, as a first step, to hire a professional property appraiser. Such an appraisal will cost around $250, but can be very useful. Firstly, you will know what your property is really worth in today's market. Therefore, you can then make an objective decision on how high to set your asking price. Of course, you probably want to set it a bit higher than the appraised value to leave some room for negotiation. On the other hand, you'll now know not to set your asking price too high so that your listing will not get stale-dated. Secondly, when it comes to negotiating with a potential buyer, you will know within what price limits you should probably stay. Unless you are working with a time issue, you certainly don't want to sell below the appraised value.

To establish the market value of your property, the appraiser will take into consideration the neighbourhood, the site description, the interior finish, the condition and layout of the unit, the age, the quality, and any improvements made to the property. The appraiser will furthermore use a combination of two methods to arrive at market value. First is the direct comparison approach, which compares your property with other units sold in the building, in the development or in the neighbourhood. Second is the cost approach, which calculates the cost to build an equal number of square feet with equal quality and standards, and then factors in the value of the land the unit sits on.

If the property appraisal comes out favourably, you now have the additional option of leaving a copy of the appraisal on the kitchen counter next to the feature sheet so that all potential buyers who do a walk-through of your unit can verify with their own eyes the true value of the property. Moreover, in your advertising on the MLS, on the Internet, or in the real estate paper, you can add a comment such as "priced at appraised value" or "priced close to appraised value."

Working with an appraiser is also recommended when you wish to move to a new principal residence and you want to transform your old residence into a rental property, but keep it in your name. As this transaction will not involve an official sale, the appraiser's value will then be the basis for future taxation.

You also will work with an appraiser when family members take over property shares belonging to other family members. In this case, there also will be no official market price established, as those shares will change hands according to internal pricing.

Advertising

There is one really easy thing you can do to speed up the sale of your property and, perhaps, obtain a better price. Before you put the property up for sale, put a lot of thought into how you advertise your property. You know the ins and outs of your property better than anyone else, and no one would put as much effort into attractive text as you. There is a lot of poor and unimaginative advertising in the marketplace, written by people who use standard formulas. You will attract more buyers with a well-composed ad, and your real estate agent will love it.

To illustrate, let us look at four ads. Ads #1 and #2 are interesting and well composed. Ads #3 and #4, which describe the same properties, lack enthusiasm and fresh ideas. Well-written and creative ads, such as ads #1 and ad #2, draw in the reader's attention and make the potential buyer want to view the property. They fulfill their purpose. Ads #3 and #4 will be read and forgotten, without invoking any interest in the potential buyer—there will most likely be no viewing unless the listing price appears to be a steal!

Ad #1 Great value here! This award-winning, 2004 building is a popular addition to Surrey's condo scene. This functional, 711-square-foot, one-bedroom-with-den unit is located on the second floor, south-west corner and features a large, wrap-around, sunny-view deck. Unit has an open floor plan and large windows with lots of natural light. Good-sized den with a large window could double as a second bedroom. The suite includes kitchen with breakfast bar, granite countertops, all appliances, in-suite laundry, electric fireplace, blinds, and secured, underground parking. Central location: walking distance to shopping, restaurants, movie theatre, parks, and recreation. Grab a cup of coffee at the coffee bar located on the ground floor of the building.

Ad #2 Welcome to 991 Clearwater Place: Sun Valley Family Home … a spacious home in Langley with potential on 0.17 acres. Minutes from excellent amenities: schools, shopping, and Goldstream trails. Over 1,800 square feet of living space with three bedrooms, two bathrooms, and family room. The west-facing yard is fully fenced with space enough to play, relax, or plant a spring garden!

Ad #3 This unit is a one bedroom and den unit. Approximately 700 square feet. Parking. Central location. Motivated seller.

Ad #4 Three-bedroom, two-bathroom, single-family house located in Langley. Fenced yard. Needs new carpets and new paint. Offers accepted.

The Deal

Together with your real estate agent, you have established the asking price. Now you are waiting for offers to come in. If you live in a region that is currently a hot market, someone may be willing to pay your asking price in full—but, this potential buyer includes the clause "subject to the sale of my own house." Inquire for how long and for how much that place has been on the market to estimate his chance for a quick sale. There are cases where you may be better off to take another offer that comes pretty close to your asking price.

In a declining market, a sale may take weeks or months. If you finally get an offer, consider it carefully. The moment you don't accept that offer, but have your real estate agent present a counteroffer, there is always the chance that the buyer may lose interest and walk away.

If market conditions are solid, on the other hand, and your real estate agent assures you that there is a good chance for more offers to come in, you can start a game of offer/counteroffer with the intention of meeting somewhere in the middle. Your real estate agent can guide you in this because he or she will be highly sensitive in picking up the vibrations underlying the negotiations. Once a good deal is within reach, get your signed acceptance of the offer back to the buyer as soon as possible to avoid a last-minute change of mind. With the Internet, the market has become a lot faster, and money is chasing opportunity at a breakneck speed. It is not unheard of that sales people in large real estate offices are available 24/7. Also, the time given by the real estate agent to accept an offer/counteroffer is becoming shorter and shorter. Know your limits in terms of price, and don't become pressured to sell at "any price." Act rationally, and don't take offers personally—especially not low offers.

It may be a good idea to avoid pressure tactics with the buyer; that is, avoid saying, "This is my final offer and this is as low as I go." The buyer may not be willing to accept your final offer and will consequently walk away. It is usually better to leave all your doors open and avoid such comments unless you are absolutely certain that the offer is as low as you will go.

When negotiating, your own timeline is also important. Have you made an offer on another property and do you need to sell right away? Or are you moving away and don't want to leave your house empty? Or, do you need the funds? If you are in a hurry for any reason, you may be willing to accept a lower offer than you would if you have the option to hold on to the property for longer. When you are selling into a balanced market and you are moving from one location to the next, interim financing may be a better option than accepting a low bid.

Competing Offers

If you are in the lucky situation of receiving more than one offer at a time, your real estate agent will present you with all the competing offers at the same time. However, you can accept only one offer or make a counteroffer to one offer. This is not an auction situation. You need to choose one offer to work with. You do that by analyzing the complete package of each of the offers: price, completion date, deposit, "subject to" clauses, and so forth. Then you respond to your best choice only.

In a competing offer situation, all the potential buyers know that they are competing with each other and will structure their offers accordingly. This ultimately means a higher sales price.

Although competing offers most likely occur when a property is newly listed, competing offers can occur any time during the entire period a property is listed for sale.

Sold!

You have found a buyer for your property. The sales contract has been signed. After years of rising real estate prices, you, too, have made a nice profit. Now you want to throw a big party and celebrate—and then move on with your new agenda. You sold, yet your real estate agent will not put "sold" on your "for sale" sign—or even remove it altogether. The real estate agent will wait at least until all "subject to" clauses in your contract have been removed. Your real estate agent will be cautious, and so should you.

Until you have received the money, do not believe anything! It has happened before: a seller thinks he has sold his property, but then the sales contract does not go through. He then has to go through the full sales process again. There is one rule that cannot be stressed enough: when it comes to real estate deals, never believe anything until you have it in writing and you have the full amount of money in your bank account.

To illustrate this with just one case: There is a prospective buyer who calls your real estate agent on the phone to remove the "subject to" conditions of the sale within the time limit for doing so. Then a few days pass and your real estate agent hears nothing from the buyer. It is rather obvious that it is very difficult to prove that this buyer removed the "subject to" conditions orally rather than in writing should the sale fall through later.

Or, there could be the case that your real estate agent confirms to you that he has received the removal of all conditions in writing. You receive a deposit of several thousand dollars that same day. However, a month or two later, on the completion date of the sale, the buyer lets you know he is still working at putting the financing together and asks for patience—or, even worse, the buyer lets you know that he can no longer afford to buy your property. You expected to receive a certain amount of money at the completion date of your contract of sale. You now will obviously be in big trouble if you have bought another property or signed any other legal document that commits your money. You may keep the buyer's deposit, which may be a significant amount, but all other damage claims can be addressed only in court by legal action against the buyer. In such a situation, which occasionally happens in a slow market, you will not get the money agreed on in your sales contract. The fastest way to reach your goal is to start all over again and find another buyer. There is usually no expense borne by the seller in case of a bad sale, but the loss of time can be significant. Again, don't spend the proceeds of a real estate sale until you have received the money, or a lender—the bank—guarantees payment on time in writing.

Of course, in a real estate market that is buzzing with activity, if any deal falls through, it will not take much effort to try again. With interest rates low and inflation in check, the outlook for the market is quite positive. One might even get a better deal the second time around as prices are still rising and demand has not yet shown a tendency to ease.

Conclusion

There are a few rules you should know about when you have your property up for sale. First and foremost, to avoid lowering the asking price significantly over time—it is better to price the property fairly from the beginning. Lowering an overly high asking price because your expectations did not materialize in time generally will provide you with a lower return than if you started out with a fair price in the beginning. By the time you realize your mistake, your property may have become stale dated, or your need to sell becomes more pressing, or you may just lose your patience. A thorough market analysis at the outset will help you prevent this type of mistake and help you set up a realistic price from the beginning. Remember, the greatest number of people who will view your home come within the first two to three weeks.

Also, it is a good idea to make your property as attractive to the potential buyer as possible: stage your home, renovate if necessary, and choose your advertising words thoughtfully. Then, when the offers come flowing in, keep a cool head and evaluate each one carefully. Don't be afraid to negotiate—the buyer expects this. And, finally, when you have found a buyer, don't celebrate until the funds have actually arrived in your bank account.

Key Points
❖ Renovations: determine what will pay off, what won't.
❖ Find a real estate agent you are comfortable working with.
❖ Do a comparative market analysis.
❖ Set a realistic price.
❖ Be thoughtful in your advertising.
❖ Stage your home.
❖ Consider each offer carefully.
❖ Negotiate.
❖ Don't spend the proceeds from the sale until the money is in the bank.

Chapter 14:

Some Final Thoughts

These days few people totally finance a first home or investment property with their own money. Using leverage will increase your buying power, but also will multiply your risks. This makes it paramount that you are well informed about which direction interest rates will take.

When you invest in real estate property with a goal to make good money, be aware that the real estate market, the stock market, and the bond market are all interconnected and depend to a large extent on the direction of interest rates. Both private mortgage financing and construction financing are highly sensitive to interest rates. In this regard, the single most important figure to keep a close eye on is the U.S. short-term interest rate, set by the Federal Reserve. Although Canada sets its rates independently, with about 80 per cent of Canadian exports going to the United States, Canadians need to keep a close eye on what is happening across the border. On September 18, 2007, the Federal Reserve cut the federal funds rate for the first time in four years from 5.25 per cent to 4.75 per cent to prevent both a recession and to counteract a growing housing slump, with record defaults in the sub prime mortgage industry, in the United States. Commercial banks are expected to follow suit by reducing their prime lending rate, lowering borrowing costs for consumers and businesses. As of June 2007, the Federal Reserve has kept the federal funds rate the same for an entire year at 5.25 per cent. Prior to June 2006, the U.S. Federal Reserve raised the federal funds rate seventeen times with the objective to counteract the economic threat of inflation. When we look back at the year 2004, the federal funds rate in the United States was at a historic low of 1 per cent.

Of course, as time goes on, the leading economic indicators will change and interest rates will be adjusted accordingly. As this information is of utmost importance, you will always see business report headlines whenever there is a Federal Reserve meeting scheduled to set these rates.

In addition to looking at what is happening across the border, how can you make a prediction in which direction mortgage rates in Canada are heading?

Mortgage rates are tied to the bond market. The bond market takes its cues from the overnight lending rates which are set by the Bank of Canada. Interest rates by themselves are a reflection of the overall economic performance of a country as well as the inflationary outlook. At present, with the Canadian economy remaining strong, but core inflation still a concern, especially in Canada's western provinces, it is expected that the Canadian central bank will keep interest rates stable for the time being.

Real estate is an integral part of a broader market; but, on the other hand, in a country as diverse as Canada, not all regions take part in the economic performance equally or at the same time. Canadian cities where the economy remains strong and unemployment remains low support a strong real estate market. The stronger the economy of a region, the more vibrant its real estate market is.

As real estate is part of the economy, real estate is cyclical. Buyers and sellers must draw their own conclusions about where in the real estate cycle they stand at any given time. Starting with the Easter holidays in spring of 2007, a high-flying Vancouver real estate agency put up its own radio frequency to advertise their properties for sale. This is just another indication that western regions are booming. Of course, this is also an inventive way to help solve a problem: many condominium towers do not allow "for sale" signs.

Some economists fear that demographics may have a downward pressure on the future real estate market. Yet, according to Statistics Canada (an agency that provides economic, social, and census data and analysis), Canada's population will grow from 32,248,600 people in 2006 to approximately 36,250,300 people in 2026, with a large part of this growth coming from immigration.[xvi]

Every year, Canada welcomes about 240,000 new immigrants, and, as these immigrants immerse themselves into the Canadian economy and join the national workforce, statistics show that most of them, within a few years, do buy their own home. On the other hand, still looking at demographics, we also have the baby boomer generation, who may downsize or upgrade into even more expensive homes, thereby keeping the housing demand level. However, what is significant is that a survey done by Century 21 shows that the baby boomers play an active role in helping their children buy their first home through financial support and guidance; for example, with a cash gift for a down payment on the first home or a financial guarantee to facilitate the purchase of a home.[xvii]

In summary, financial knowledge is always an asset. It opens doors and lets you seize opportunities. Real estate knowledge is no different. The purpose of this book is to provide you with the information you need. The book does not intend to push you in one direction or the other. This being said, owning real estate will always be a pillar of any sound financial planning to secure your own living standard and establish a rock solid foundation for a happy and financially worry-free retirement. Real estate prices in Canada have more than tripled in the past twenty-five years. From this perspective, investing in real estate and owning your own home make good financial sense. As is typical for any type of asset allocation, timing is one of the most important factors. Yet, there are many strategies and considerations that can help you to make the right decisions and reach your goals faster. So if you have decided to buy, my sincere hope is that this book contains just the right information and serves as an excellent and complete reference for you to make your real estate investments a success story and to enhance your quality of life with a fabulous home.

REFERENCES

i   May 31, 2007. Canadian Real Estate Association.

ii   June 1, 2007. CIBC World Markets. Statement.

iii   Statistics Canada.

iv   Canadian Real Estate Association. Statistics.

v   Canadian Real Estate Association.

vi   Centre for Global Energy Studies.

vii   CREA, TREB, OMREB, CREB, EREB, RE/MAX. Statistics. January 25, 2007. *Times Colonist.*

viii   Can West News Service. Beauchesne, Eric. September 20, 2006. *Times Colonist.*

ix   January 2007. RE/MAX. Report.

x   June 20-27, 2007. GfK Roper Public Affairs and Media. Study.

xi   Canadian Real Estate Association. August 4, 2007. *The Globe and Mail.*

xii   Royal Bank. Survey.

xiii   Canadian Broadcasting Corporation (CBC). *Report on Business News.*

xiv   Canada Mortgage and Housing. June 6, 2007. Edmonton Rental Market Report.

xv   Can West News Service. Toneguzzi, Mario. March 16, 2007. *Times Colonist.*

xvi   Statistics Canada.

xvii   Century 21. Survey.

978-0-595-44318-5
0-595-44318-4

Printed in the United States
96518LV00005B/46-132/A